The People of
NORTH EAST
SCOTLAND
at Home and Abroad
1800 - 1850

By
David Dobson

Copyright © 2022
by David Dobson
All Rights Reserved

Published for Clearfield Company by
Genealogical Publishing Company
Baltimore, Maryland
2022

ISBN: 9780806359458

INTRODUCTION

This book identifies people from the old counties of Nairnshire, Morayshire, Banffshire, Aberdeenshire, and Kincardineshire, of the period 1800 to 1850. The information derives from a wide range of contemporary sources such as court records, contemporary newspapers and journals, monumental inscriptions, and documents found in archives. The main clans or families found in this region were Rose, Grant, Dunbar Brodie, Innes, Gordon, Leslie, Ogilvie, Keith, Forbes, Hays, Barclay, Fraser, Skene, Farquharson, Arbuthnott, Burnett, Irvine, and Douglas.

The society and economy of North East Scotland was rural and depended on industries such as farming, fishing, whaling distilling, quarrying, and forestry. There were several small burghs, notably Stonehaven, Peterhead, Fraserburgh, Banff, Elgin, Nairn, Fochabers, Buckie and Old Meldrum, most of which were semi-autonomous and had burgesses and other civic organisations. The most important burgh in the region was, and is, Aberdeen, which I covered in *The People of Aberdeen at Home and Abroad, 1800-1850*. The North East population were largely Presbyterian, with a significant Episcopalian presence and a few Roman Catholic enclaves.

For those wishing to put their family history into context the best sources are the Old Statistical Reports of the 1790s and the New Statistical Reports compiled between 1832 and 1845. These Reports were produced by parish ministers and covered a wide range of subjects such as geography, education, history, the economy, agriculture, shipping, population, and religion. These Reports are available on the website of the National Library of Scotland. The best collections of local histories are in the library of the Aberdeen and North East Scotland Family History Society. The single best history of emigration from the region is the two-volume *Emigration from North East Scotland* by Marjory Harper, published in Aberdeen in 1980.

David Dobson, Dundee, Scotland, 2022

REFERENCES

ACA   Aberdeen City Archives

AJ   Aberdeen Journal, series

ANY   St Andrew's Society of New York

AOB   Annals of Banff

AR   Acadian Recorder, series

BA   Officers of the Bengal Army

BBR   Banff Burgess Roll

BM   Blackwood's Magazine, series

BPP   British Parliamentary Papers, series

CG   City Gazette, series

DC   Dundee Courier, series

DPCA   Dundee, Perth, & Cupar Advertiser, series

EBR   Elgin Burgess Roll

ENES   Emigration from North East Scotland

F   Fastii Ecclesiae Scoticanae

GM   Gentleman's Magazine, series

HJ   Halifax Journal, series

HT   Halifax Times, series

KCA   King's College, Aberdeen

MCA   Marischal College, Aberdeen

NARA   National Archives Records Administration

NBC   New Brunswick Courier, series

NRS   National Records of Scotland

OSA   Old Statistical Account

PC   Perth Courier, series

POD   Post Office Directory, series

PSAS   Proceedings of Society of Antiquaries of Scotland, series

S   The Scotsman, series

SAA   Society of Advocates in Aberdeen

SG   Scottish Guardian, series

SM   Scots Magazine, series

TML   The McLeods

TNA   The National Archives

UPC   United Presbyterian Church

WSP   Washington State Pioneers

Castle Invercauld, Aberdeenshire

Highland games at Braemar Castle, Aberdeenshire

Castle Fraser, Aberdeenshire

Ellon Castle, Aberdeenshire

Skene Castle

Nineteenth-century Peterhead, showing the old brickwork in the background

NOTICE TO PASSENGERS.
FIRST SHIP FOR QUEBEC.
The well-known fast-sailing coppered Ship, regular Trader,
BRILLIANT,
550 Tons Burthen,
ALEX. BARCLAY, Commander,
Will clear at the Custom-house for QUEBEC on Thursday August, and sail on Friday the 10th August. Has excellent accommodation for Cabin and Steerage Passengers, her between decks being above six feet.
For Freight or Passage, apply to
WILLIAM DUTHIE, Footdee
Aberdeen, 31st July, 1832.

Newspaper advertisement for passengers to Quebec

For Quebec, from Peterhead.
THE Fine Oak-built and Fast-sailing Ship, "**JOSEPH GREEN,**" 353 Tons Register, JAMES VOLUM, Commander, will be on the berth, at Peterhead, for Goods and Passengers for Quebec, direct.

This fine Vessel will sail from Peterhead about the 10th of May next, and proceed to Cromarty; will be on the berth there, about the 18th May; and be dispatched from thence about the 28th of May, to Scrabster Roads, and Lochinver; and will remain for two days at each of the above places, for the embarkation of Passengers.

This vessel is well adapted for Passengers, having 6 feet 6 inches height between decks. She will be fitted up in a superior manner, and will have First and Second Cabin apartments—restricted to a limited number of Passengers. A Surgeon has been appointed for the ship.

Apply, at Peterhead, to Mr WILLIAM VOLUM, Manager; or Captain VOLUM, on board; and for Cromarty, Scrabster Roads, and Lochinver, to Mr DUNCAN M'LANNAN, Emigrant Agent, Inverness.
Peterhead, 4th April, 1842.

Vessel "Jospeh Green" sailing for Quebec

PEOPLE OF NORTH EAST SCOTLAND, 1800-1850

ABERNETHIE, MARGARET, daughter of Dr Abernethie in Banff, married Colquhoun Grant from Jamaica, in Banff on 28 January 1798. [GM.68.168]

ADAM, JOHN, a cooper or mariner at Elias Green, Peterhead, was accused of housebreaking and theft in 1822. [NRS.AD14.22.130]

ADAM, ROBERT, agent for the North of Scotland Bank in Macduff in 1849. [POD]

ADAMSON, ALEXANDER, a fisherman in Banff, then in the Seatown of Cullen, Banffshire, was ordered to be apprehended for not fulfilling a contract, in 1812. [Annals of Banff.i.351]

ADAMSON, JOHN, the elder, in Strichen, Aberdeenshire, testament, 1809, Comm. Aberdeen. [NRS]

ADAMSON, WILLIAM, a fisherman in Banff, then in the Seatown of Cullen, Banffshire, was ordered to be apprehended for not fulfilling a contract, in 1812. [Annals of Banff.i.351]

ADAMSON, WILLIAM, a merchant from Banff, died in Brighton, Melbourne, Victoria, Australia, on 30 April 1875. [AJ.6652]

ADDISON, ALEXANDER, born in Keith, Banffshire, was educated at Marischal College, Aberdeen, in 1777, a schoolmaster in Aberlour, Banffshire, son in law of Reverend Grant in Elgin, Moray, later a judge in Washington County, America, died in Pittsburgh, Pennsylvania, on 24 November 1807. [F.6.394][SM.70.398]

AINSLIE, ROBERT FORREST, born 28 June 1811, died Glasgow, 8 June 1862, sons William Allan, born 9 January 1839, died Hamilton, Canada West, 2 March 1840, Robert John Gordon, born 18 June 1843, died 13 June 1848 in Hamilton, Canada West. [Rothes gravestone]

AITKEN, JAMES, born 1839, son of John Aitken and his wife Jane Smith, died n New Zealand on 17 December 1865. [Braemar gravestone, Aberdeenshire]

ALEXANDER, ANDREW SNODGRASS MUIR, in Chicago, Illinois, heir to his uncle George Lewis William Forbes, a solicitor in Banff, who died on 4 January 1862, re property in Fordyce, Aberdeenshire. [NRS.S/H]

ALEXANDER, CHARLES, in Strathend of Cruden, Aberdeenshire, testament, 1817, Comm. Aberdeen. [NRS]

ALEXANDER, GEORGE, son of George Alexander a merchant in Banff, was educated at Marischal College around 1830, later became a Member of the Canadian Senate. [MCA]

ALEXANDER, JAMES, from Banff, graduated MA from King's College, Aberdeen, on 27 March 1795. [KCA]

ALEXANDER, JAMES, an elder of the parish of Banff in 1834. [AOB.ii.116]

ALEXANDER, JOHN, sr., a mariner in Catterline, Kinneff, Kincardine, testament, 1807, Comm. St Andrews. [NRS]

ALEXANDER, JOHN J. J., of St Lucia in the British West Indies, married May Reid, daughter of James Reid a shipmaster in Fraserburgh, Aberdeenshire, in Bath on 31 August 1813, [SM.75.798]

ALEXANDER, JOHN, was accused of discharging firearms at Macduff, Gamrie, Banff, in 1837. [NRS.JC26.1837.62]

ALEXANDER, MARY, born 1842, daughter of John Alexander and his wife Margaret Hay, wife of George McLennan, died in Queensland, Australia, on 2 September 1892. [Portlethen gravestone, Kincardineshire]

ALEXANDER, R., agent for the Aberdeen Town and County Bank in Peterhead, Aberdeenshire, in 1849. [POD]

ALEXANDER, WILLIAM, agent for the North of Scotland Banking Company in Peterhead, Aberdeenshire, in 1849. [POD]

ALLAN, ALEXANDER, a writer in Edinburgh, son of James Allan a merchant in Garmouth, Moray, was admitted as a Notary Public on 2 July 1793, died in 1801. [NRS.NP2.35.71]

ALLAN, ALEXANDER, born 1798 in Moray, a house-carpenter who was naturalised in South Carolina on 16 August 1847. [NARA.M1183/1]

ALLEN, ALEXANDER, born 1825, son of John Allen and his wife Helen, died in Jamestown, South Australia, on 14 December 1879. [Inveravon gravestone, Banffshire]

ALLAN, GEORGE, a farm servant in Cairnbanno, New Deer, Aberdeenshire, was accused of assault and robbery in 1846. [NRS.AD14.46.5]

ALLAN, JAMES, from Inverkeithnie, Banffshire, graduated MA from King's College, Aberdeen, on 29 March 1792, later minister at Newhills. [KCA]

ALLAN, JAMES, from Banff, graduated MA from King's College, Aberdeen, in March 1832, later a minister in Campbeltown, Argyll. [KCA]

ALLAN, JAMES, born 1832, eldest son of Francis Allan a merchant tailor in Old Meldrum, Aberdeenshire, a Corporal of the Waikato Militia, was accidentally shot at St John's Redoubt, Papatoitoi, New Zealand, on 19 October 1863. [AJ.6055]

ALLAN, WILLIAM, son of Alexander Allan at the brick-kilns on the Links, was apprenticed to Alexander Ross, a merchant in Aberdeen, in 1787. [ACA]

ALLAN, WILLIAM, a shipmaster in Burghead, a sasine, 1791. [NRS.RS.Elgin.299]; testament, 1795, Comm. Moray. [NRS]

ALLAN, WILLIAM, a fisherman in Johnshaven, Kincardineshire, died on 20 December 180-, aged 92 years, husband of Isobel Leys, born 1716, died 1778. [Benholm gravestone, Kincardineshire]

ALLAN, WILLIAM, born 1806, son of James Allan and his wife Margaret Winton, died in Tasmania, Australia, on 13 March 1857. [Fettercairn gravestone, Kincardineshire]

ALLAN, ..., master of the George of Banff trading between Hamburg, Aberdeen and Leith in 1799. [AJ.2699]

ALLARDYCE, ALEXANDER, Episcopalian minister in Elgin, Moray, from 1760 to 1799, and in Old Deer, Aberdeenshire, from 1799 until 1816.

ALLARDYCE, ALEXANDER, from Banff, graduated MA from King's College, Aberdeen, on 29 March 1793, later minister at Forgue, Aberdeenshire. [KCA]

ALLARDYCE, FRANK, son of Reverend William Allardyce and his wife Nancy Cruickshank in Rhynie, Aberdeenshire, was educated at Marischal College in 1830s, joined the Honourable East India Company, died in Madras, India, on 6 June 1841. [F.6.330][MCA]

ALLARDYCE, HUGH DUFF, born 1843, son of Samuel Allardyce and his wife Jessie McQueen, died in Melbourne, Victoria, Australia, on 12 October 1860. [Leochel Cushnie gravestone, Aberdeenshire]

ALLARDYCE, JOSEPH, son of Samuel Allardyce in Tulloch Venus, Tough, Aberdeenshire, was apprenticed to Alexander Thomson a cooper in Aberdeen in 1792. [ACA]

ALLARDYCE, WILLIAM, son of Samuel Allardyce in Tulloch Venus, Tough, Aberdeenshire, was apprenticed to William Still jr. a cooper in Aberdeen in 1794. [ACA]

ALLARDYCE, WILLIAM, a teacher of English in Banff in 1805. [AOB.ii.206]

ALLISTER, ALEXANDER, beadle of the parish church in Banff until 1836. [AOB.ii.119]

ANDERSON, AGNES, born 1750, widow of Reverend Andrew Youngson minister of Aberdour, died in the Manse od Strichen, Aberdeenshire, in 1825. [AJ.22.5.1825]

ANDERSON, ALEXANDER, son of Alexander Anderson in Drumblade, Aberdeenshire, was educated at King's College, Aberdeen, in 1825, a surgeon in America. [KCA]

ANDERSON, ALEXANDER, a surgeon in Peterhead, Aberdeenshire, testament, 1806, Comm. Aberdeen. [NRS]

ANDERSON, ALEXANDER, born 1770, a farmer in Avalds, died 20 May 1834, husband of Ruth Mitchell, born 1780, died 11 January 1828. [Banff gravestone]

ANDERSON, ALEXANDER, born 1841, son of John Anderson a carpenter from Hardgate of Clatt, Aberdeenshire, later in Cashel Street, Christchurch, New Zealand, died at Stillwater Creek, N.Z. on 3 December 1861. [AJ.5982]

ANDERSON, ALEXANDER ROSE MUNRO, son of John Anderson, born 1789, died 1840, and his wife Mary Ross, born 1806, died 1871, died in Broken Hill, Australia. [Kincardine Ardgay gravestone]

ANDERSON, ALEXANDER, son of Alexander Anderson a farmer in Elgin, Moray, at Marischal College in 1850s, later in Huntingdon, Canada. [MCA]

ANDERSON, ANN, in New Leeds of Strichen, Aberdeenshire, testament, 1821, Comm. Aberdeen. [NRS]

ANDERSON, BASIL, minister of Old Deer, Aberdeenshire, from 1779 until his death in 1797, testament, 1798, Comm. Aberdeen. [NRS]

ANDERSON, CHARLES, in Jamaica, died in 1816, brother of William Anderson in Loanhead, Coldstone, Aberdeenshire, Comm. Aberdeen. [NRS]

ANDERSON, DAVID, son of David Anderson in Alves, Moray, a merchant in Fredericton, New Brunswick, probate, 1797, N.B.

ANDERSON, GEORGE, born 1725, feuar in Macduff, Banffshire, died 8 May 1792, father of George Anderson born 1757, in Headston of Cullen, died 7 June 1832, his wife Isabella Joss, born 1761, died 14 May 1838. [Banff gravestone]

ANDERSON, HERCULES, born 30 November 1843, son of William Anderson and his wife Rosalind Duthie, died in Blenheim, New Zealand, on 26 April 1899. [Benholm gravestone, Kincardineshire]

ANDERSON, JAMES, a bank agent in Peterhead, Aberdeenshire, versus George Minty in 1832. [NRS.CS271.52702]

ANDERSON, Dr JAMES, in St Kitts, later in Midmiln of Cruden, Aberdeenshire, in 1800. [NRS.RGS.132.34.35]

ANDERSON, JAMES, son of Alexander Anderson in Kemnay, Aberdeenshire, graduated MA from Marischal College in 1817, later a surgeon in the Service of the East India Company. [MCA]

ANDERSON, JAMES, a merchant from Forres, Moray, died in Augusta, Georgia, on 19 July 1823. [BM.14.624]

ANDERSON, JAMES, master of the Lady Duff of Banff in 1793. [AJ.2381]

ANDERSON, JAMES, a skipper in Macduff, testament, 1804, Comm. Aberdeen. [NRS]

ANDERSON, JAMES, sr., a merchant in Peterhead, Aberdeenshire, testament, 1823, Comm. Aberdeen. [NRS]

ANDERSON, JAMES, MD, son of James Anderson and his wife Elspet Gow in Scroggie Mill, Elgin, Moray, settled in Melbourne, Victoria, Australia, by 1856. [NRS.S/H; RGS.132.34.35]

ANDERSON, JOHN, a farmer in the Greens of Strichen, Aberdeenshire, testament, 1804, Comm. Aberdeen. [NRS]

ANDERSON, JOHN, master of the Lively of Peterhead Aberdeenshire, trading between Fort William and Inverness in 1811. [NRS.E504.17.8]

ANDERSON, JOHN JAMES, editor of *The Gipsland Times*, son of Reverend Andrew Anderson, minister of Crathie and Braemar, Aberdeenshire, died in Sale, Gippsland, Australia, on 30 June 1872. [AJ.9506]

ANDERSON, LEWIS CHALMERS, born 1833, a teacher from Banff, died in Beaufort West, Cape of Good Hope, South Africa, on 1 September 1861. [AJ.5936]

ANDERSON, MARY, daughter of George Anderson in Aberchirder, Banffshire, married Francis L. Farquharson from Baltimore, Maryland, in New York on 10 June 1867. [AJ.6233]

ANDREW, Mrs ELIZA, born 1806 in Keith, Banffshire, wife of John Andrew a clothier, emigrated via Aberdeen to Quebec on 27 August 1842, settled in Brockville on 27 October 1842, died there on 5 December 1842. [AJ.4959]

ANDREW, GEORGE, from Huntly, Aberdeenshire, graduated MA from King's College, Aberdeen, on 1 April 1860. [KCA]

ANDREW, THOMAS, from Gamrie, Banffshire, graduated MA from King's College, Aberdeen, in March 1851, later was a surgeon in the Service of the East India Company. [KCA]

ANGUS, GEORGE, born 12 October 1794, son of Reverend Alexander Angus and his wife Katherine Mair in Botriphnie, Banffshire, a physician in the Honourable East India Company Service, died in Aberdeen on 7 April 1872. [F.6.302]

ANNAND, ALEXANDER, a sailor aboard the whaling ship Robert of Peterhead, Aberdeenshire, off Greenland and the Davis Strait in 1794. [NRS.E508.94.8.10]

ANNAND, ROBERT, an apprentice aboard the whaling ship Robert of Peterhead, Aberdeenshire, off Greenland and the Davis Strait in 1791. [NRS.E508.94.8]; and steersman, as above, in 1794. [NRS.E508.94.8.10]

ARBUTHNOTT, ANN, fourth daughter of James Arbuthnott a merchant in Peterhead, Aberdeenshire, testament, 1791, Comm. Aberdeen. [NRS]

ARBUTHNOTT, CHRISTIAN, in Kirkton of Peterhead, Aberdeenshire, daughter of James Arbuthnott in Rora, testament, 1796, Comm. Aberdeen. [NRS]

ARBUTHNOTT, CHRISTIAN, widow of Thomas Fraser a shipmaster in Peterhead, Aberdeenshire, testament, 1816, Comm. Aberdeen. [NRS]

ARBUTHNOTT, GORDON, youngest son of William Arbuthnott of Dens, died in Berryden, Port Natal, South Africa, on 31 July 1856. [AJ.5678]

ARBUTHNOTT, JAMES, of Dens, born 1741, died in Peterhead, Aberdeenshire, in 1823. [AJ.19.3.1823]

ARBUTHNOTT, JAMES, born 1757, late postmaster of Peterhead, Aberdeenshire, died there in 1829. [AJ.9.2.1829]

ARBUTHNOTT, JAMES, a white thread manufacturer in Peterhead, Aberdeenshire, second son of James Arbuthnott a merchant there, testament, 1791, Comm. Aberdeen. [NRS]

ARBUTHNOTT, JAMES, son of William Arbuthnott of Dens a gentleman in Peterhead, a student at Marischal College around 1830, emigrated to Natal, South Africa. [MCA]; a Member of the Legislature Council, died at Umzinto Lodge, Nata, on 4 May 1861. [AJ.5926]

ARBUTHNOTT, THOMAS, with his son William Arbuthnott, were co-owners of the herring-buss Polly of Peterhead, Aberdeenshire, in 1792, [NRS.E508.94.9.56]; testament, 1794, Comm. Aberdeen. [NRS]

ARBUTHNOTT, THOMAS, of Nether Kinmundy, Aberdeenshire, died in Peterhead, Aberdeenshire, in 1826. [AJ.11.3.1826]

ARBUTHNOTT, WILLIAM, born 1766, son of Robert Arbuthnott and his wife Mary Urquhart in Haddo-Rattray, Aberdeenshire, was a planter in Carriacou, the Grenadines, from 1783, returned to Scotland by 1804. [PSAS.114.482]

ARBUTHNOTT, DALGARNO, and Company, woollen cloth manufacturers in Peterhead, and Arbuthnott, in 1790s. [OSA]

ARBUTHNOTT, GRANT, and Company, cotton cloth manufacturers in Peterhead, and Arbuthnott, in 1790s. [OSA]

ARGO, GEORGE, from Tarves, Aberdeenshire, graduated MA from King's College, Aberdeen, in March 1851. [KCA]

ASHER, JOHN GORDON, born on 31 May 1837, son of Reverend William Asher and his wife Katherine Forbes in Inveravon, Banffshire, a surgeon major in Bombay, India. [F.6.345]

AUCHINACHIE, JOHN, born 1769, a farmer at Backielay, died 9 April 1834, son of Alexander Auchinachie, [1715-1791], a farmer at Backielay. [Marnoch gravestone, Banffshire]

AUSTINE, JAMES, son of the postmaster of Fettercairn, Kincardineshire, died in Windsor Forrest, Demerara, on 2 August 1839. [AJ.4787]

BAIN, ROBERT, born in Garmouth, Moray, on 16 April 1836, died 10 March 1891. [St George's gravestone, Port Elizabeth, South Africa]

BAIRNSFATHER, STENHOUSE, a teacher in the Infant School in Wilson's Institution, Banff, in 1843. [AOB.ii.126]

BALFOUR, HENRY, a merchant, was ordained as an elder in Banff on 21 March 1841. [AOB.ii.122]

BALFOUR, JAMES, son of Henry Balfour a merchant in Banff, was educated at Marischal College, Aberdeen, in 1854, later a banker in Sydney, New South Wales, Australia. [MCA]

BALNEAVES, ISABEL, from Links of Arduthy, Fetteresso, Kincardineshire, a prisoner in Aberdeen Tolbooth, was banished from Scotland on 27 April 1799. [NRS.JC11.43]

BANDEEN, BARBARA, from Alford, Aberdeenshire, settled in Ohio by 1833, married William Coutts, settled in Red Oak, Cedar County, Iowa, died in 1848. [ENES.I.252]

BANDEEN, JOHN, from Alford, Aberdeenshire, died in Red Oak Grove, Cedar County, Iowa, on 16 January 1854. [ENES.I.252]

BANDEEN, RACHEL, from Alford, Aberdeenshire, settled in Ohio by 1833, married William Coutts after 1848, settled in Red Oak, Cedar County, Iowa, [ENES.I.252]

BANNERMAN, WILLIAM, a schoolmaster in Peterhead, Aberdeenshire, testament, 1814, Comm. Aberdeen. [NRS]

BARBER, WILLIAM MCLEOD, born 31 May 1827 in Fochabers, Moray, son of Thomas Barber and his wife Madeline McLeod, emigrated to Newhaven, Connecticut, educated at Yale University, a minister, died in 1889 in Malden, Massachusetts. [TML.2.39]

BARCLAY, CHARLES GEORGE, son of Charles Barclay a farmer in the parish of St Andrew, Moray, a student at Marischal College in 1830s, later a merchant in the West Indies. [MCA]

BARCLAY, GEORGE, son of John Barclay a farmer in Echt, Aberdeenshire, was apprenticed to William Barclay a shoemaker in Aberdeen in 1792. [ACA]

BARCLAY, JAMES, from the Mearns, graduated MA from King's College, Aberdeen, on 27 March 1795. [KCA]

BARCLAY, JOHN ALEXANDER, son of Charles Barclay a farmer in St Andrews Llanbryde, Moray, a student at Marischal College in 1840s, later a civil servant in the West Indies. [MCA]

BARCLAY, PATRICK, from Auchterless, Aberdeenshire, graduated MA from King's College, in March 1846, later in New Zealand. [KCA]

BARCLAY, WILLIAM, son of Charles Barclay a farmer in St Andrews Llanbryde, Moray, a student at Marischal College in 1840s, later a merchant in the West Indies. [MCA]

BARLAS, WILLIAM, minister of the Whitehill Antiburgher Church, Aberdeenshire, from 1779 to 1797, then settled in New York as a teacher of the Classics and a bookseller, died 7 January 1817. [UPC]

BARNETT, WILLIAM, son of Alexander Barnett a fisherman in Nigg, Kincardineshire, graduated MA from Marischal College in 1817, later schoolmaster of Nigg. [MCA]

BARRACK, ALEXANDER, in Ellon, Aberdeenshire, father of Mrs Barbara Reid, who died in Gloucester, Massachusetts, on 13 July 1877. [AJ.13.7.1877]

BARRIE, WILLIAM MORISON, born 1852, son of James Barrie and his wife Jean Steven, died in Sydney, New South Wales, Australia, on 21 September 1891. [Fetteresso gravestone, Kincardineshire]

BARRON, ALEXANDER, MA, born 1745 in Kincardineshire, was educated at Marischal College, Aberdeen, and at the University of Edinburgh, a Loyalist in 1776, died 9 January 1819. [Old Scots gravestone, Charleston, S.C.] [TNA.AO13.90.60]

BARRON, JANE, daughter of George Barron, [1795-1861], and his wife Jean Durward, [1806-1891], died in Queensland, Australia. [Strachan gravestone, Kincardineshire]

BARRON, JOHN, son of William Barron in Insch, Aberdeenshire, was apprenticed to Alexander Barron a baker in Aberdeen in 1791. [ACA]

BARTLETT, PATRICK, from Banff, settled in Carriacou by Grenada, later in London, executor of Joseph Cumming in 1799. [NRS.CC8.8.131]

BARTLETT, WILLIAM, treasurer of the parish of Banff in 1834. [AOB.ii.116]

BAXTER, ANN, born 1830, daughter of William Baxter, a feuar in Fochabers, Moray, and his wife Ann Logie, died in Canada in 1890. [Bellie gravestone, Moray]

BAYNE, JAMES BENTLEY, late of Melbourne, Victoria, Australia, son of James Bayne MD, died in Nairn on 4 December 1857. [AJ.6256]

BAYNE, RONALD, in Nairn, graduated MA from King's College, Aberdeen, in March 1840, also graduated MD from King's College, Aberdeen, on 10 April 1845, later a surgeon in the Service of the East India Company. [KCA]

BEATON, JOHN, from Mortlach, Banffshire, a sailor on <u>HMS Camel</u>, testament, 1805, Comm. Aberdeen. [NRS]

BEATON, PATRICK, born 8 June 1825 in Lethanty, Fyvie, Aberdeenshire, son of William Beaton and his wife Margaret Cowieson, graduated MA from King's College, Aberdeen, in March 1844, later a minister in Mauritius and in Paris, died on 11 October 1904. [KCA][F.7.535]

BEATON, WILLIAM, from Longside, Aberdeenshire, graduated MA from King's College, Aberdeen, later minister of St Andrews in Grenada. [KCA]

BEATTIE, ALEXANDER, from Lumphanan, Aberdeenshire, graduated MA from King's College, Aberdeen, on 1 April 1860, later a schoolmaster in Lumphanan, and a minister in Newcastle. [KCA]

BEATTIE, JAMES, a servant at the Mains of Arbuthnott, Kincardineshire, a prisoner in Aberdeen Tolbooth, was banished from Scotland on 28 May 1798. [NRS.JC11.43]

BEATTIE, JOHN, born 1809, youngest son of Dr Beattie in Insch, Aberdeenshire, died in Aurora, Wisconsin Territory, on 28 March 1839. [AJ.4766]

BEATTIE, WILLIAM COPLAND, son of James Beattie a surveyor in Australia, was educated at Marischal College, Aberdeen, in 1859. Later a sheep farmer in Australia. [MCA]

BEATTIE, WILLIAM, born 1843 in Old Deer, Aberdeenshire, son of James Beattie in Benwells, a stonecutter who died in St Louis, Missouri, on 15 August 1876. [AJ.13.9.1876]

BEGG, GEORGE, a farmer, [1764-1856] and his wife Jane Walker, [1764-1834], parents of William Begg, born 1802, died in Guatamala 1826. [Glen Tannar gravestone, Aberdeenshire]

BEGG, JOHN, born 1812, a merchant in Aberchirder, Banffshire, died 17 June 1897, husband of Jane Findlator, born 1814, died 24 August 1900. [Marnoch gravestone, Banffshire]

BELL, WILLIAM, born 1737, blacksmith to the Earl of Aboyne, died in January 1823, husband of Margaret Masson, born 1764, died in February 1849. [Aboyne gravestone, Aberdeenshire]

BENNETT, JAMES GORDON, born 1795 in Enzie, Banffshire, son of James Bennett and his wife Janet Reid, emigrated to Nova Scotia in 1819, moved to New York in 1822, founder of the *New York Herald*, died 2 June 1872. [ANY]

BENTON, JOSEPH, born 1841, son of William Benton and his wife Margaret Joss, died in Townsville, Queensland, Australia, on 2 April 1880. [Alford gravestone, Aberdeenshire]

BERRY, ROBERT, formerly a barrister in Hamilton, Upper Canada, was granted the lands of Torphin on 30 July 1856. [RGS.257.20.78]

BETHUNE, Dr GEORGE, in Tobago, was admitted as a burgess of Banff in 1800. [BBR]

BETHUNE, JOSEPH, of Dornock, born 21 December 1781, a Major of the 78th Regiment, died 2 April 1837. [St Andrew's Episcopal Church in Banff]

BIGGAR, WALTER, an elder of the parish of Banff in 1834. [AOB.ii.116]

BIRNIE, ALEXANDER, in Kinbog, Fraserburgh, Aberdeenshire, testament, 1803, Comm. Aberdeen. [NRS]

BIRNIE, ALEXANDER, from Banff, graduated MA from King's College, Aberdeen, on 29 March 1805, later schoolmaster in Lumphanan, Aberdeenshire. [KCA]

BIRNIE, BATHIA, in Fraserburgh, Aberdeenshire, widow of William Walker in the Mains of Techmuiry, Aberdeenshire, testament, 1815, Comm. Aberdeen. [NRS]

BIRNIE, or DAVISON, ELIZA, a widow in Fraserburgh, Aberdeenshire, married William Baxter, a widower from Dundee, on 17 December 1797. [Fraserburgh Episcopal Records]

BIRNIE, GEORGE, born 1777, a Sergeant of the 1st Battalion of the Royal Artillery for 21 years, died in Old Meldrum, Aberdeenshire, on 22 May 1865, husband of Lilly Gray, born 1783, died 9 March 1869. [Daviot gravestone]

BIRNIE, RICHARD, born 1730, died in Banff on 12 January 1812, husband of Margaret Philip, born 1736, died 14 August 1820. [Banff gravestone]

BISSET, SAMUEL, born 1793 in Aberdeenshire, a saddler, and his wife Anne, born 1793 in Banffshire, who were naturalised in New York on 20 April 1821. [N.Y Court of Common Pleas]

BLACK, ALEXANDER LESLIE, born 1813 in Forres, Moray, son of Charles Black and his wife Ann Leslie, died in New Orleans, Louisiana, on 9 October 1837. [AJ.4692]

BLACK, JAMES, born 1763, a Member of His Majesty's Council of Nova Scotia, died at Summerhill, Aberdeenshire, on 4 September 1823. [CG.23.10.1823]

BLACK, JAMES, a shipmaster in Peterhead, the log book of the schooner Naughton 1814-1815. [NRS.CS96.4041]

BLACK, JOHN, son of Robert Black a grain merchant in Newburgh, Aberdeenshire, was educated at Marischal College, Aberdeen, in 1852, later a banker in Melbourne, Victoria, Australia. [MCA]

BLACK, WILLIAM, son of John Black in Old Machar, Aberdeenshire, a student in Marischal College, graduated MA in 1794. [MCA]

BLACK, WILLIAM, son of William Black of Cloghill, Aberdeenshire, a student in Marischal College in 1790s. [MCA]

BLACKIE, WILLIAM, a farmer in Netherton, married Margaret Cooper in Fraserburgh, Aberdeenshire, on 28 December 1799. [Fraserburgh Episcopal Records]

BLAIR, JAMES, born 7 November 1792, son of James Blair, a merchant in Stonehaven, Kincardineshire, and his wife Elizabeth Taylor-Imrie, a soldier of the Bengal Army from 1809 to 1847, died at sea on 12 August 1847, Lieutenant Colonel of the 5th Native Infantry. [BA.1.159]

BLAKE, ALEXANDER, a vintner in Banff in 1849. [Annals of Banff.i.368]; born 1798, a merchant in Banff, died 1 May 1863, husband of Cecilia Ronald, born 1810, died 2 May 1857, parents, of Alexander Blake, born 1834, drowned in the SS Mauritius off the coast of Ireland on 6 November 1872. [Banff gravestone]

BLAKE, ALEXANDER, son of William Blake a farmer in Longside, a student at Marischal College in 1854, later a Free Church minister in Madras, India, then in New Zealand. [MCA]

BLANE, ROBERT, a Lieutenant Colonel in the Service of the East India Company, a sasine in Elgin, Moray, in 1792. [NRS.R.S.Elgin.328]

BLUNTACH, JOHN, in Forres, Moray, father of James Bluntach who settled in Hastings, Minnesota, by 1872. [NRS.S/H]

BLYTH, JOHN, born 1774, son of John Blyth a merchant in Old Meldrum, Aberdeenshire, died in Falmouth, Jamaica, in 1809. [PC.61]

BODIE, JOHN, a shipmaster in Peterhead, Aberdeenshire, testament, 1812, Comm. Aberdeen. [NRS]

BONNAR, ANDREW, schoolmaster of Nigg, Aberdeenshire, father of George Bonnar a sailor in the Royal Navy, in 1799. [NRS.S/H]

BOYD, GORDON, a messenger in Peterhead, Aberdeenshire, versus Alexander Farquhar a merchant in Glasgow, a decreet, 1815. [NRS.CS42.13.74]

BOYD, Mrs JANE, born 1765 in Elgin, Moray, died in Halifax, Nova Scotia, on 23 November 1837. [AR.25.11.1837]

BRAND, GEORGE MURRAY, from Arbuthnott, Kincardineshire, graduated MA from King's College, Aberdeen, in March 1839, later was the British Consul in Loanda. [KCA]

BRANDER, JOHN, of Pitgaveny, heir to his uncle Alexander Brander of Kinedward, 16 March 1795. [Records of Elgin.i.503]

BRANDER, JOHN, a merchant in Elgin, Moray, was granted a lease of Gallow Hill, there on 18 May 1799. [Records of Elgin I.509]

BRANDER, ROBERT and WILLIAM BRANDER, agents for the British Linen Company in Elgin, Moray, in 1849. [POD]

BRANDER, WILLIAM, born 1780, younger son of Provost Brander of Elgin, Moray, died on St Michael's Island on 23 October 1803. [DPCA.74]

BRANDS, Dr ROBERT, youngest son of James Brands of Ferry Hill, [1703-1780], and his wife Ann Stewart, [1710-1793], [gravestone, Aberdeen] [GM.XII.582.170]

BRANDS, ROBERT ABERCROMBY, a writer in Forres, Moray, later in Sugar Grove, Warren County, Pennsylvania, a sasine. 1838. [NRS.RS.Elgin.254]

BREBNER, JOHN, son of James Brebner a blacksmith in Fordoun, Kincardineshire, at Marischal College around 1853, later Minister of Education in the Orange Free State, South Africa. [MCA]

BREBNER, JOHN, son of John Brebner a contractor in Forgue, Aberdeenshire, was educated at Marischal College, Aberdeen, in 1854, a Lieutenant of the 79th Highlanders, later in New Zealand and New South Wales, Australia. [MCA]

BREBNER ROBERT, from Tarland, Aberdeenshire, graduated MA from King's College, Aberdeen, in March 1851. [KCA]

BREBNER, SIBELLA, daughter of Alexander Brebner of Learney, died in Aberdeen on 26 June 1820. [SM.86.191]

BREBNER, WILLIAM, son of William Brebner, [1743-1827], a farmer at Boat of Bridge, Moray, and his wife Margaret Simpson, [1752-1820], a physician in Jamaica. [SG]

BREMNER, Mrs ELSPETH, aged under 50, a farmer's widow, with four children aged under 14, from Kennethmont, Aberdeenshire, emigrated to South Australia in 1848. [BPP.11.164]

BREMNER, GEORGE, from Marnoch, Banffshire, graduated MA from King's College, Aberdeen, in March 1840, later a government teacher at the Cape of Good Hope, South Africa. [KCA]

BREMNER, JAMES, from Banff, graduated MA from King's College, Aberdeen, on 30 March 1797. [KCA]

BREMNER, JAMES, born 26 December 1831 in Rhynie, Aberdeenshire, son of John Bremner and his wife Margaret Cran, married Abigail Clark Freeman in Chicago, Illinois, in 1845, settled in Iowa, died in Delta, Washington, on 19 March 1887. [WSP]

BREMNER, JOHN, born 1792, son of Joseph Bremner, a feuar in Fochabers, Moray, and his wife Mary Allan, settled in the Bahamas after the wreck of the warship *Laurustinus* as a merchant in Nassau, New Providence, died on 30 August 1818. [Bellie gravestone, Moray]

BREMNER, JOHN, son of Robert Bremner a farmer in Boharm, Banffshire, was educated at Marischal College in 1815, later a surgeon in Keith, Banffshire. [MCA]

BREMNER, ROBERT, born 1845 in Fochabers, Moray, was educated at King's College, Aberdeen, author of 'Travels in Russia' [London 1839], died in 1872. [AOB.ii.127]

BROCKIE, or BROWN, JANET, in Fraserburgh, Aberdeenshire, testament, 1814, Comm. Aberdeen. [NRS]

BRODIE, JAMES, son of Walter Brodie a farmer in Fordoun, Kincardineshire, graduated MA from Marischal College in 1817, later a Free Church minister. [MCA]

BRODIE, JOSEPH, from Leith, a Captain of the Royal Navy, residing in Peterhead, Aberdeenshire, testament, 1816, Comm. Aberdeen. [NRS]

BRODIE, LOUISA, from Moray, wife of H. Cotton a surveyor, in Van Diemen's Land from 1843 to 1850. [NRS.NRAS.0021]

BRODIE, MARGARET, in Bangalore in the East Indies, grand-daughter of the Brodie of Brodie, died 27 January 1825, an inventory, 1831, Edinburgh. [NRS]

BROTCHIE, JOHN ALEXANDER, born 22 October 1849 in Kintore, Aberdeenshire, son of John Brotchie, was educated at Aberdeen University, a minister in New South Wales from 1883 until his death on 2 September 1908. [F.7.588]

BROWN, Dr GORDON, born on 2 July 1784, son of Reverend Brown and his wife Isabella Ord in New Spynie, Moray, was educated at Marischal College from 1799 to 1802, a physician in Demerara, died there on 16 July 1813, father of Ann Brown in Elgin, Moray, 1835. [NRS.PS3.15.149] [F.6.4][EA.5192.13]

BROWN, JAMES, son of Alexander Brown in Knockollochy, Chapel of Garioch, Aberdeenshire, died at Montego Bay, Jamaica, on 12 August 1848. [AJ.4.10.1848]

BROWN, J., a weaver in Banff, donated into the poor fund of Banff in 1836. [AOB.ii.119]

BROWN, PETER, born 1766, son of Robert Brown a farmer at Bridgend of Knockandoch in the parish of Lochell, Moray, died in Raleigh, North Carolina, on 26 October 1833. [AJ.4481]

BROWN, WILLIAM, born 1749, a manufacturer and stampmaster in Banff, died 19 September 1829, husband of Janet Simpson, born 1742, died 11 September 1841. [Banff gravestone]

BROWN, WILLIAM, from Ardnamuddle, Aberdeenshire, died in Brownsville, Illinois, on 1 July 1849. [AJ.5299]

BRUCE, ALEXANDER, in Fraserburgh, Aberdeenshire, sequestration papers, 1848. [NRS.CS279.332]

BRUCE, DANIEL, born 1823 in Grantown-on-Spey, Moray, fourth son of John Bruce, died in Sacramento, California, on 18 August 1874. [S.9720]

BRUCE, GEORGE, born 1835, son of William Bruce and his wife Margaret....., chief engineer aboard the steamship Feelong, was lost at sea off the coast of China on 23 September 1874. [Aberdour gravestone, Aberdeenshire]

BRUCE, JEAN, widow of Robert Montgomery in Old Deer, Aberdeenshire, an inventory, 1818, Comm. Aberdeen. [NRS]

BRUCE, JOHN, born 1794, a seaman from Fraserburgh, Aberdeenshire, aboard the whaling ship the Oscar of Aberdeen when bound for Greenland, was shipwrecked and drowned off Aberdeen on 1 April 1813. [Nigg gravestone, Aberdeenshire]

BRUCE, JOHN, [1825-1895], and his wife Christian Ritchie, [1829-1871], parents of William Andrew Bruce, born 1854, died in Harford, California, on 12 October 1896. [Monymusk gravestone, Aberdeenshire]

BRUCE, JOSEPH, a merchant in Fraserburgh, Aberdeenshire, married Margaret Murdoch, in Fraserburgh on 15 September 1796. [Fraserburgh Episcopal Records]

BRUCE, LOUISA, born 22 June 1795 in Spynie, Moray, son of Reverend Alexander Brown and his wife Isabella Ord, married William Willox of the Ordnance Department, died in Sierra Leone, Africa, on 21 March 1826. [F.6.407]

BRUCE, PETER, born in Inverurie, Aberdeenshire, a merchant who died in New York on 21 December 1796. [EEC.12291]

BRUCE, ROBERT, born in Inverurie, Aberdeenshire, a merchant who died in New York on 28 November 1796. [EEC.12291]

BRUCE, ROBERT, born 1831, son of William Bruce and his wife Margaret......, chief engineer aboard the P.& O's steamship Ravenna, died at sea and was buried at Aden on 15 July 1881. [Aberdour gravestone, Aberdeenshire]

BRUCE, WILLIAM, born 1799, a blacksmith and ironfounder, died 18 July 1884 at Sauchentree, Aberdour, husband of Margaret......, born 1797, died 27 February 1860. [Aberdour gravestone, Abrdeenshire]

BRUCE WILLIAM ROBERTSON, son of George Bruce a farmer in New Deer, Aberdeen, graduated MD from Marischal College in 1861, later in Queenstown, Cape Colony, South Africa. [MCA]

BUCHAN, ALEXANDER, [1], born 1785, a seaman from Inverallochy, Aberdeenshire, aboard the whaling ship the Oscar of Aberdeen when bound for Greenland, was shipwrecked and drowned off Aberdeen on 1 April 1813. [Nigg gravestone, Aberdeenshire]

BUCHAN, ALEXANDER, [2], born 1788, a harpooner from Peterhead, Aberdeenshire, aboard the whaling ship the Oscar of Aberdeen when bound for Greenland, was shipwrecked and drowned off Aberdeen on 1 April 1813. [Nigg gravestone, Aberdeenshire]

BUCHAN, CHARLES FORBES, son of Peter Buchan a printer in Peterhead, was educated at Marischal College 1831-1835, later minister of Fordoun, Kincardineshire, graduated DD from Jefferson College in USA. [MCA]

BUCHAN, CHARLES, a farmer in Keyhead, St Fergus, Aberdeenshire, died on 8 April 1868, uncle of William Buchan at Sturgeon Bay, Wisconsin. [NRS.SH.1897]

BUCHAN, GEORGE, born 1784, a harpooner from Peterhead, Aberdeenshire, aboard the whaling ship the Oscar of Aberdeen when bound for Greenland, was shipwrecked and drowned off Aberdeen on 1 April 1813. [Nigg gravestone, Aberdeenshire]

BUCHAN, JEAN, in Ludquharn, Old Deer, Aberdeenshire, testament, 1803, Comm. Aberdeen. [NRS]

BUCHAN, JOHN, third son of Thomas Buchan of Auchmacoy, Aberdeenshire, was apprenticed to a writer, was admitted to the Society of Writers to the Signet in 1782, died in Jamaica in 1793. [WS]

BUCHAN, JOHN, born 1768, a seaman from Inverallochy, Aberdeenshire, aboard the whaling ship the Oscar of Aberdeen when bound for Greenland, was shipwrecked and drowned off Aberdeen on 1 April 1813. [Nigg gravestone, Aberdeenshire]

BUCHAN, PETER, son of Peter Buchan a printer in Peterhead, was educated at Marischal College in 1820s, later a medical practitioner, a West India merchant, graduated Ph.D. from Jena, Germany. [MCA]

BUCHANAN, Miss, mistress of the Banff Boarding and Day School in 1822. [AOB.ii.206]

BUCK, ANDREW, son of Joseph Buck a cartwright at Tollahill, was apprenticed to Alexander Anderson a shoemaker in Aberdeen in 1790. [ACA]

BUDON, JANET, wife of John Budon in Nairn, a victim of theft in 1825. [NRS.AD14.25.227]

BUNYAN, JOHN, born 1751, a minister of the Whitehill, [Antiburgher] Church from 1798 to his death on 20 December 1821. [UPC]; husband of Janet Ireland. [New Deer gravestone, Aberdeenshire]

BURGESS, JAMES, in Demerara and Essequibo, son of William Burgess a tenementer in Rothes, Moray, who died in November 1831. [NRS.S/H.1867]

BURGESS, JOHN, master of the Alexander of Portsoy Banffshire, trading between Fort William and Inverness in 1807. [NRS.E504.17.8]

BURNETT, ALEXANDER, son of John Burnett of Elrick, Aberdeenshire, died in Union near Grenada on 18 June 1790. [S]

BURNETT, GEORGE, husband of Isabel Lunan in Fraserburgh, Aberdeenshire, a member of the Aberdeenshire Militia in 1807. [ACA.AS.AMI.6.1.1]

BURNETT, JAMES, in Batavia, was admitted as a burgess of Banff in 1771. [BBR]

BURNETT, JAMES, son of James Burnett of Monbuddo, Fordoun, Kincardineshire, a student at Marischal College around 1850, later a Captain of the Madras Army in India. [MCA]

BURNETT, MARGARET, daughter of John Burnett of Elrick, Aberdeenshire, married Norman McLeod from Montreal, Quebec, in Aberdeen on 26 July 1811. [SM.73.237]

BURNETT, WILLIAM, born 1827, from Banff, died in Greenwich, New York, on 9 May 1854. [AJ.12.7.1854]

BURNS, JOHN, husband of Margaret Davidson, in Fraserburgh, Aberdeenshire, a member of the Forfarshire Militia in 1804. [ACA.AS.AMI.6.1.1]

BURR, JAMES, born 1818, in Pitblain, died 7 May 1890, husband of Jane Stronach, born 1824, died 12 August 1887. [Daviot gravestone]

BUTCHART, THOMAS, a fisherman in Gourdon, testament, 1818. Comm. St Andrews. [NRS]

CADENHEAD, JOHN, born 1842, fifth son of William Cadenhead, a farmer in Cloghill, Newhills, Aberdeenshire, died in Tuaranga, New Zealand, on 11 October 1873. [AJ.6577]

CADGER, PETER, husband of Mary Pennie in Fraserburgh, a member of the Aberdeenshire Militia in 1806. [ACA.AS.AMI.6.1.1]

CAIRD, JAMES, in Farskane, Cullen, Banffshire, father of John Hay Caird, born 1856, died at Hartwell House, Kiama, New South Wales, Australia, on 1 February 1885. [S.13010]

CALDER, CHARLES, from Banff, graduated MA from King's College, Aberdeen, on 29 March 1793. [KCA]

CALDER, WILLIAM, in Hartfield, Connecticut, heir to his uncle Alexander Calder of Asswanlie, Aberdeenshire in 1809. [NRS.S/H]

CAMERON, ANDREW ROBERTSON, MD, late of Banchory and Tarland, Aberdeenshire, died in Kurrygong, Sydney, New South Wales, Australia, in 1876. [AJ.6729]

CAMERON, ELIZABETH MILNE, eldest daughter of Charles Cameron, formerly a book seller in Huntly, Aberdeenshire, married William Nisbet an engineer, in New York on 25 April 1871. [S.8670]

CAMERON, HUGH, steersman on the <u>Robert of Peterhead</u> whaling off Greenland or the Davis Strait in 1794. [NRS. E508.94.8/10]

CAMERON, JAMES, born 9 June 1787 in Dalvey, Cromdale, died at Boyndlie House on 10 March 1863. [Aberdour gravestone, Aberdeenshire]

CAMERON, JAMES, from Logie Coldstone, Aberdeenshire, graduated MA from King's College, Aberdeen, in March 1846, later a Free Church minister in Sydney, New South Wales, Australia. [KCA]

CAMERON, PETER, from Banff, graduated MA from King's College, Aberdeen, on10 March 1801, later schoolmaster in Botriphnie, Banffshire. [KCA]

CAMERON, PETER, a solicitor in Banff in 1825. [Annals of Banff.i.351]

CAMERON, WILLIAM, born 1827, son of James Cameron, died at Aberdour House, Aberdeenshire, on 6 January 1844. [Aberdour gravestone, Aberdeenshire]

CAMPBELL, COLIN, St Ann's, Middlesex, Jamaica, heir of John Bryce Campbell in St Vincent appointed Duncan Campbell in Nairn and Lewis Dunbar of Grange in Moray, as his attornies concerning the estate of Delvis, Fort George, Nairnshire, in 1797. [NRS.RD4.263.273]

CAMPBELL, DONALD, born 1844, died in Honolulu, Hawaii, on 3 August 1900. [Crathie gravestone, Aberdeenshire]

CAMPBELL, DONALD, baptised on 27 June 1806 in Nairn, son of Hugh Campbell and his wife Jane Falconer, died in North Carolina on 11 November 1885. [Raleigh gravestone, N.C.]

CAMPBELL, DUNCAN, a surgeon in the Service of the Honourable East India Company at Fort Marlborough, Sumatra, father of Margaret Campbell, testament, 1796, Comm. Aberdeen. [NRS]

CAMPBELL, Mrs GRASSIE, born 1763 in Grandholm near Aberdeen, died in Halifax, Nova Scotia, on 7 September 1843. [Halifax Times, 12.9.1843]

CAMPBELL, HANNAH, born 1810 in Nairn, died in North Carolina on 14 January 1840. [Raleigh gravestone, N.C.]

CANTLAY, JAMES, son of James Cantlay a farmer in Ellon, Aberdeenshire, a student at Marischal College in 1850s, later a planter in Ceylon. [MCA]

CARDNO, JOHN, in Turriff, Aberdeenshire, a letter to Alexander Jolly in 1814. [NRS.CH12.30.107]

CARL, JOHN, a fisher in Cairnbulg, Aberdeenshire, testament, 1822, Comm. Aberdeen. [NRS]

CARMICHAEL, JANE, probably from Nairn, settled in New South Wales before 1850. [NRS.S/H]

CARR, ANNIE, youngest daughter of Robert Carr a farmer on the Hill of Mennie, Aberdeenshire, married Arthur Littlejohn a millwright, in Tokomairiro, New Zealand, on 30 July 1874. [AJ.6618]

CARRUTH, W. B., from Broughty Ferry, Angus, a teacher of English in Banff from 1846 to 1847. [AOB.ii.207]

CASSIE, JAMES, a prisoner in Aberdeen Tolbooth, was banished from Scotland for seven years on 16 April 1796. [NRS.JC11.42]

CASSIE, WILLIAM, born 1799, an innkeeper in Banff, died 8 November 1834, husband of Jane Cruickshank, born 1802, died 19 May 1848. [Banff gravestone]

CATTENACH, CHARLES, born 1803, a farmer from Ballater, Aberdeenshire, died in Durham, Sandhurst, Australia, on 23 September 1874. [AJ.6622]

CATTENACH, DUNCAN, born 1843, youngest son of Duncan Cattenach in Toldow, Glen Muick, Ballater, Aberdeenshire, died at Bruce's Creek, Australia, on 9 October 1866. [AJ.6223]

CATTO, ALEXANDER, in Peterhead, Aberdeenshire, a sequestration petition, 1841. [NRS.CS279.442]

CENTER, ALEXANDER, a merchant in Fraserburgh, Aberdeenshire, testament, 1822. [NRS]

CHALMERS, ALEXANDER SCOTT, born in Aberdeenshire, died in Rutland Vale, St Vincent, on 9 January 1863. [AJ.18.2.1863]

CHALMERS, GEORGE, a house carpenter from Strichen, Aberdeenshire, died in Panama on his way from California to Alabama in March 1852. [AJ.7.7.1852]

CHALMERS, JOHN, born 1746, died 13 February 1825, husband of Isabell Scott, born 1746, died 6 August 1826. [Aberdour gravestone, Aberdeenshire]

CHALMERS, JOHN, from New Deer, Aberdeenshire, graduated MA from King's College, Aberdeen, in March 1848, later a missionary in China. [KCA]

CHALMERS, L., agent in Fraserburgh, Aberdeenshire, for the Bank of Scotland in 1849. [POD]

CHAPPELL, JOHN, from Aberdeenshire, emigrated to New York in 1833, settled in Iowa. [ENES.252]

CHARLES, ALEXANDER S., born 18 August 1845 in Stonehaven, Kincardineshire, married Mary Jane McAvoy in Ferndale, Whatcom, Washington Territory, on 13 May 1874, died in Bellingham, Whatcom, in 1922. [WSP]

CHEYNE, GEORGE, born 25 July 1802, son of William Cheyne, a farmer in Auchterless, Aberdeenshire, and his wife Elizabeth Harper, was educated at King's College, Aberdeen, graduated MA, from 1818 to 1822, later was a minister in Hamilton, Ontario. [KCA]

CHEYNE, MARGARET, born 1749, daughter of Charles Cheyne a merchant in Edinburgh, and niece of Dr George Cheyne of Esslemont, Aberdeenshire, died in Lunenburg, Nova Scotia, on 8 January 1821. [AR.20.1.1821]

CHISHOLM, ADAM, a prisoner in Stonehaven Tolbooth, Kincardineshire, was banished from Scotland in 1799. [NRS.JC11.44]

CHISHOLM, ALEXANDER, a farmer at the Haughs of Turriff Aberdeenshire, versus Alexander Scott, a distiller at Mount Blairy Distillery, Turriff, in 1830. [NRS.CS271.717]

CHISHOLM, ALEXANDER, son of Alexander Chisholm a farmer in the Haughs of Turriff, Aberdeenshire, was educated at Marischal College, Aberdeen, in 1828, later a missionary in the South Seas. [MCA]

CHISHOLM, ANNE, a prisoner in Stonehaven Tolbooth, Kincardineshire, was banished from Scotland in 1799. [NRS.JC11.44]

CHIVAS, ROBERT, in Upper Adiel of Strachan, Kincardineshire, testament, 13 July 1815, Comm. Aberdeen. [NRS]

CHRISTIAN, PETER, a writer in Stonehaven, Kincardineshire, son of Angus Christian an apothecary there, was admitted as a Notary Public on 15 November 1798, died on 27 July 1855. [NRS.NP2.36.99]

CHRISTIE, GEORGE, from Banff, graduated MA from King's College, Aberdeen, on 29 March 1792. [KCA]

CHRISTIE, JAMES, born 1754, a fisherman in Stonehaven, Kincardineshire, died in 17 March 1838. [Cowie gravestone, Kincardineshire]

CHRISTIE, JAMES, born 1792, a seaman from Peterhead, Aberdeenshire, on the whaling ship the <u>Oscar of Aberdeen</u> bound for Greenland, was shipwrecked and drowned off Aberdeen on 1 April 1813. [Nigg grave, Aberdeenshire]

CHRISTIE, JAMES, MA, in Huntly, Aberdeenshire, graduated MD from King's College, Aberdeen, on 30 July 1840 [KCA]

CHRISTIE, JAMES, from Kildrummy, Aberdeenshire, graduated MA from King's College, Aberdeen, in March 1846, later a missionary in Constantinople and in Canada. [KCA]

CHRISTIE, JOHN, from Banff, graduated MA from King's College, Aberdeen, on 29 March 1793. [KCA]

CHRISTIE, JOHN, in the Mains of Artamford, New Deer, Aberdeenshire, testament, 1817, Comm. Aberdeen. [NRS]

CHRISTIE, JOHN, MA, in Huntly, Aberdeenshire, graduated MD from King's College, Aberdeen, on 29 April 1841. [KCA]

CLARK, ALEXANDER, born 1820, died in Teremny, Rothiemay, on 20 June 1880, husband of Margaret Ogilvie, born 1823, died 28 January 1856. [Marnoch gravestone, Banffshire]

CLARKE, Reverend DONALD, from Paisley, Renfrewshire, a missionary in Banff in 1840. [AOB.ii.122]

CLARK, GEORGE, from Ellon, Aberdeenshire, graduated MA from King's College, Aberdeen, in March 1850, later a schoolmaster in Dundee. [KCA]

CLARK, JAMES, in Netherhill, St Fergus, Aberdeenshire, in 1796. [NRS.CS96.43]

CLARK, JAMES, a mariner in Banff, master of the sloop <u>George of Banff</u>, testament, 1823, Comm. Aberdeen. [NRS]

CLARKE, JAMES, born 1776 in Banffshire, died in Windsor, Nova Scotia, on 31 August 1837. [AR.30.9.1837]

CLARK, JOHN, born 1784, in Raemore, died in February 1854, husband of Ann Ogilvie, born 25 February 1794, died 7 March 1887. [Marnoch gravestone, Banffshire]

CLARK, JOHN MOIR, son of John Clark a merchant in Elgin, Moray, a student at Marischal College in 1850s, later a physician in Sarawak. [MCA]

CLARK, WILLIAM, born 1788 in Ballater, Aberdeenshire, died in Jersey City, New York, on 10 February 1851. [AJ.19.3.1851]

CLARK, WILLIAM, born 1809, a traveling brush vendor, and Janet Thomson, were accused of the murder of his wife Elizabeth, at Craighall, Ellon, Aberdeenshire, in 1849. [NRS.AD14.49.250]

CLARK, WILLIAM, born 1817, a master mariner, late of Peterhead, Aberdeenshire, died in Hobart Town, Australia, on 7 March 1862. [AJ.5968]

CLAYTON, Captain, born 1791, died in Miramachi, New Brunswick, on 18 May 1818. [Banff gravestone]

CLERIHEW, Reverend PATRICK, MA, born 1809, formerly a minister in Cookney, Fetteresso, Kincardineshire, died in Maryborough, Queensland, Australia, in 1868. [AJ.6323]

CLUB, ALEXANDER, a shipmaster in Fraserburgh, husband of Jean Taylor, a sasine, 1790. [NRS.RS.Aberdeen.892]

CLUB, ALEXANDER, born 1767 in Fraserburgh, Aberdeenshire, a merchant who was naturalised in South Carolina on 25 September 1802. [NARA.M1183/1]

CLUNAS, JAMES, born 1809, son of William Clunas and his wife Janet Mackay, late in New Orleans, Louisiana, died in Nairn on 2 January 1888. [Wardlaw gravestone, Inverness]

COBBAN, GEORGE, from Banffshire, graduated MD from King's College, Aberdeen, on 26 July 1847. [KCA]

COCK, WILLIAM, a fresh or green-man on the whaling ship the Robert of Aberdeen bound for Greenland and the Davis Strait in 1794. [NRS.E508.94.8.10]

COLLIE, JOSEPH, from Elgin, Moray, graduated MA from King's College, Aberdeen, in March 1844, later with the Victoria Insurance Office, in Melbourne, Victoria, Australia. [KCA]

COLLINS, THOMAS, from Kincardineshire, graduated MD from King's College, Aberdeen, on 5 August 1852. [KCA]

COMBIE, JAMES, died in Montreal, Quebec, in 18... [Banff gravestone]

CONNON, C. W., teacher in the Madras School of Banff in 1837. [AOB.ii.207]

CONNON, JAMES, from Aberdeenshire, died 8 May 1865, father of Alexander Connon in Cremore, County Wexford, Ireland. [NRS.S/H]

COOK, WILLIAM, born 1825 in New Pitsligo, Aberdeenshire, died in Albany, New York, on 27 August 1861. [AJ.18.9.1861]

COOPER, ARTHUR, a writer in Edinburgh, son of John Cooper a shoemaker in Findhorn, Moray, was admitted as a Notary Public on 7 July 1798. [NRS.NP2.36.181

COOPER, CHARLES, son of John Cooper a farmer in Kincardine O'Neil, Aberdeenshire, graduated 1848 from Marischal College, later a Professor at the Christian College in Madras, India. [MCA]

COOPER, ELIZABETH, wife of William Scorgie a fish dealer in Inverurie, Aberdeenshire, was accused of wilful fire-raising in 1828, case not proven. [NRS.JC26.1828.77]

COOPER, ISABELLA, born 1813 in Aberdeenshire, died in Halifax, Nova Scotia, on 24 November 1839. [AR.30.11.1839]

COPLAND, JOHN, born 1812 in Ellon, Aberdeenshire, died in Tufton Hall, Grenada, on 16 May 1870. [AJ.22.6.1870]

CORDINER, JAMES, from Banff, graduated MA from King's College, Aberdeen, on 29 March 1793. [KCA]

CORDINER, JOHN, in Burnhillock, Cruden, Aberdeenshire, testament, 1811, Comm. Aberdeen. [NRS]

CORDINER, Mrs, born 1748, widow of Reverend Charles Cordiner, died in Peterhead, Aberdeenshire, in 1834. [AJ.15.11.1834]

CORMACK, GEORGE, a fresh or green-man on the whaling ship the Robert of Aberdeen bound for Greenland and the Davis Strait in 1791. [NRS.E508.94.8]

CORMACK, JAMES, a skipper in Stonehaven, testament, 1821, Comm. St Andrews. [NRS]

CORMACK, WILLIAM, a fresh or green-man on the whaling ship the Robert of Aberdeen bound for Greenland and the Davis Strait in 1791. [NRS.E508.94.8]

CORMACK, WILLIAM, son of James Cormack a farmer in Rayne, Aberdeenshire, was educated at Marischal College in 1840s, later a schoolmaster in Aberdeen, thereafter, a minister of the Dutch Reformed Church in Burgersdoff, Cape Colony, South Africa. [MCA]

COULL, JOHN, born 1818, died at Mill of Cranna on 2 February 1899, husband of Elspet Murray, born 1815, died 30 December 1905. [Marnoch gravestone, Banffshire]

COULL, GEORGE, from Rathven, Banffshire, graduated MA from King's College, Aberdeen, in March 1850, later a minister in Smyrna, Canada. [KCA]

COURAGE, JAMES, son of James Courage at Silverburn, was apprenticed to John Lamb a wright in Aberdeen in 1790. [ACA]

COUTTS, ADAM, born 1817, from Oldtown Croft, Insch, Aberdeenshire, died in Pleasant Township, Iowa, on 4 June 1875. [AJ.14.7.1875]

COUTTS, ELIZABETH, wife of Robert Pirie from Keig, Aberdeenshire, died in Red Oak Grove, Cedar County, Iowa, on 29 May 1853. [AJ.19.10.1853]

COUTTS, JOHN, a surgeon in Fraserburgh, Aberdeenshire, died 20 June 1843, father of James Cock Coutts in Hong Kong, formerly a wine merchant in Calcutta, India. [NRS.S/H.1861]

COUTTS, PETER, born 1817, a merchant tailor in Banff, died 18 July 1876, husband of Susan McHattie, born 1813, died 31 August 1858. [Banff gravestone]

COUTTS, WILLIAM, emigrated from Aberdeenshire to Ohio in 1834, settled in Red Oak township, Cedar County, Iowa, in 1837. [ENES.1.252]

COW, ALEXANDER, a farmer in Peterhead, Aberdeenshire, testament, 1812, Comm. Aberdeen. [NRS]

COW, WILLIAM, a carpenter in Peterhead, Aberdeenshire, later in Newton of Kinmundy, testament, 1816, Comm. Aberdeen. [NRS]

COWIE, ALEXANDER, son of Andrew Cowie in Fochabers, Moray, was educated at Marischal College around 1815, later a merchant in Aberdeen. [MCA]

COWIE, DAVID, born 1826 in Cairney, Aberdeenshire, son of Reverend William Cowie, died on St Vincent on 8 January 1878. [AJ.26.1.1878]

CRABB, WILLIAM, born 1768, a boxmaker, died in Laurencekirk, Kincardineshire, on 24 November 1825. [SM.97.127]

CRAGIE, ALEXANDER, a shipmaster in Johnshaven, Kincardineshire, son of ...... Cragie and his wife Elspet Blews [1739-1800]. [Benholm gravestone, Kincardineshire]

CRAGIE, Mrs JANET, born 1744, died 1803, wife of John Cragie a shipmaster in Johnshaven, Kincardineshire. [Benholm gravestone, Kincardineshire]

CRAIG, JOHN, born 1788, son of Thomas Craig and his wife Helen Young, died in Albany, New York, on 11 January 1832. [Llanbryde gravestone, Moray]

CRAIK, SAMUEL, born 1750, schoolmaster in Aberdour for 53 years, died 7 July 1820, husband of Robina Panton, born 1758, died 22 February 1831. [Aberdour gravestone, Aberdeenshire]

CRAIK, WILLIAM, son of Samuel Craik schoolmaster of Aberdour, Aberdeenshire, graduated MA from Marischal College in 1817, later a farmer in Aberdour. [MCA]

CRAMMOND, JOHN, born 1829, from Peterhead, Aberdeenshire, died in Melbourne, Victoria, Australia, on 1 February 1862. [AJ.5964]

CREIGHTON, Captain GEORGE, born 1839 in Peterhead, Aberdeenshire, died in Melbourne, Victoria, Australia, on 3 October 1869. [AJ.6361]

CRIVES, WILLIAM, son of William Crives at Silverburn, was apprenticed to William Michie a wright in Aberdeen in 1791. [ACA]

CROCKETT, GEORGE, son of James Crockett a shepherd in Fettercairn, Kincardineshire, was educated at Marischal College, Aberdeen, in 1855, later was a schoolmaster in Australia. [MCA]

CROLL, Reverend ROBERT, born 1739, died at the Manse of Bervie, Kincardineshire, on 3 June 1820. [SM.86.190]

CROMBIE, ALEXANDER, son of George Crombie of Netherley, a student at Marischal College in the 1830s, later Colonel of the Madras Cavalry in India. [MCA]

CRUICKSHANK, ALEXANDER, eldest son of Dr Cruickshank in the Haughs of Corsie, died in Nickerie, Surinam, on 13 September 1820. [SM.86.383] [S.4.195] [AJ.4769]

CRUICKSHANK, CHARLES WATT, son of Dr William Cruickshank in Turriff, Aberdeenshire, was educated at Marischal College, Aberdeen, in 1859, later settled in Queensland, Australia. [MCA]

CRUICKSHANK, DANIEL, born 1757 in Moray, died in Charleston, South Carolina, on 17 November 1837. [Old Scots gravestone, Charleston, S.C.]

CRUICKSHANK, ELSPET, a victim of crime in 1837. [NRS.JC26.1837.62]

CRUICKSHANK, GEORGE, born 3 June 1793 in Rhynie, Aberdeenshire, son of Robert Cruickshank and his wife Janet Paterson, emigrated to Quebec in July 1817, settled in Laurens, South Carolina, in 1818, naturalised there on 14 April 1819. [SC.Archives.mf.69; Laurens Court Roll, 60]

CRUIKSHANK, GEORGE, agent of the North of Scotland Banking Company in Banff in 1849. [POD]

CRUICKSHANK, JAMES, from Banff, graduated MA from King's College, Aberdeen, on 26 March 1790. [KCA]

CRUICKSHANK, JAMES, a farmer in Tonkshill, New Deer, Aberdeenshire, a benefactor of King's College, Aberdeen, on 14 December 1813. [KCA]

CRUICKSHANKS, JAMES, born 1787 in Banffshire, died in Halifax, Nova Scotia, on 6 March 1838. [AR.10.3.1838]

CRUICKSHANK, JOSEPH, born 1847, youngest son of John Cruickshank in Knauchland, Rothiemay, Aberdeenshire, died in Melbourne, Victoria, Australia, on 22 May 1871. [AJ.6453]

CRUICKSHANK, WILLIAM, born in June 1760, son of Theodore Cruickshank and his wife Jane Allen in Boynsmill, emigrated to Jamaica in 1781, later a carpenter in New York, 1831. [ANY]

CRUICKSHANKS, WILLIAM, baptised on 25 September 1774 in Knockando, Moray, son of William Cruickshank and his wife Janet McDonald, emigrated to Charleston, South Carolina, in 1793, a shoemaker who was naturalised in Charleston on 15 August 1805, died on 20 October 1834. [NARA.M1183.1] [Old Scots gravestone, Charleston, S.C.]

CRUICKSHANK, WILLIAM, son of James Cruickshank a farmer in Forgue, Aberdeenshire, a student at Marischal College around 1821, later a merchant in Aberdeen. [MCA]

CRUICKSHANK, WILLIAM, son of James Cruickshank a blacksmith in Fyvie, Aberdeenshire, graduated MA from Marischal College in 1838, later schoolmaster of Old Deer, and a Presbyterian minister in Canada. [MCA]

CRUICKSHANK, WILLIAM, from Turriff, Aberdeenshire, graduated MD from King's College, Aberdeen, on 11 June 1845. [KCA]

CUMINE, CHARLES, son of Peter Cumine a shipowner in Fraserburgh, Aberdeenshire, at Marischal College in 1850s, later a merchant in Shanghai, China. [MCA]

CUMINE, THOMAS JONES, fourth son of Archibald Cumine of Auchry, Aberdeen, died in Demerara on 8 February 1820. [BM.7.231]

CUMMING, GEORGE, a writer in Banff, husband of Elizabeth Fraser, born 1819, died 16 December 1853. [Banff gravestone]

CUMING, THOMAS, in Demerara, sold his lands of Harvie, Moray, to Sir James Grant in 1800. [NRS.RD3.287.129; RD3.288.1]

CUSHNIE, ALEXANDER, in Kingston, Surrey County, Jamaica, an assignation in favour of Patrick Cushnie in Stonehaven, Kincardineshire, and his wife Ann Stratton, in 1821. [NRS.RD5.214.245]

CUSHNY, ARTHUR, eldest son of Reverend Cushny in Oyne, Aberdeenshire, died in Trinidad in 1811. [SM.73.637]

CUSHNIE, THOMAS STRATTON, in Jamaica, heir to his aunt Ann Cushnie or Burnes in Stonehaven, Kincardineshire, in 1819. [NRS.S/H]

CUSHNIE, WILLIAM, son of John Cushnie in Glashmore, was apprenticed to William Seton a baker in Aberdeen in 1794. [ACA]

CUTHBERT, JOHN, from Marykirk, Kincardineshire, residing in St John's, Newfoundland, will dated 7 April 1825, Newfoundland

DALLAS, ALEXANDER, a farmer of Newton Park, Auldearn, Nairn, was accused of forgery in 1837. [NRS.AD14.37.7]

DALRYMPLE, WILLIAM, son of James Dalrymple in Fraserburgh, Aberdeenshire, a student at Marischal College around 1824, later a surgeon who died in Trelawney, Jamaica, on 31 March 1860. [MCA][AJ.9.5.1860]

DARGUE, ANDREW, a boatbuilder in Peterhead, Aberdeenshire, testament, 1805, Comm. Aberdeen. [NRS]

DAUN, JAMES, junior, at Hillockhead of Glass, Turriff, Aberdeenshire, was accused of assault in 1818. [NRS.AD14.18.219]

DAVIDSON, A., agent in Inverurie for the North of Scotland Bank in 1849. [POD]

DAVIDSON, ADAM, second son of S. Davidson MD in Wartle, Aberdeenshire, married Cecilia Gaden, second daughter of William Gaden, in Rockhampton, Australia, on 29 April 1864. [AJ.6084]

DAVIDSON, AGNES, daughter of John Davidson in the Mains of Cairnbrogie, Tarves, Aberdeenshire, married James B. Aiken of Callao in Lima, Peru, on 2 September 1867. [AJ.6249]

DAVIDSON, ALEXANDER, in Ardclach, Nairn, a victim of murder in 1824. [NRS.AD14.17.69]

DAVIDSON, CHARLES, son of John Davidson of Tillychetly, was educated at King's College, Aberdeen, from 1790 to 1794, a physician in Grenada, died in St George's on 2 October 1804. [KCA.2.371][MCA]

DAVIDSON, DUNCAN, a writer in Aberdeen, son of John Davidson of Tillichetly, Aberdeenshire, was admitted as a Notary Public on 5 March 1794, died on 8 December 1849. [NRS.NP2.35.131]

DAVIDSON, GEORGE, born 1764, son of James Davidson, [1725-1781], and his wife Margaret Watt, [1724-1823], a merchant in Old Deer, died 4 April 1833. [New Deer gravestone, Aberdeenshire]

DAVIDSON, JAMES, a printer in Banff, husband of Ellen Susanna Valder, born 1777, died 2 July 1823. [Banff gravestone]

DAVIDSON, JOHN, a farm servant in Rora, Longside, Aberdeenshire, was accused of assault and robbery in 1846. [NRS.AD14.46.5]

DAVIDSON, LEWIS GORDON, son of William Davidson a farmer in Belmont, was educated at Marischal College, Aberdeen, in 1854, later a physician in Goulburn, New South Wales, Australia. [MCA]

DAVIDSON, ROBERT, born 1838, youngest son of Charles Davidson of the Gordon Arms Inn, Huntly, Aberdeenshire, died in Wilmington, North Carolina, on 24 August 1863. [AJ.6069]

DAVIDSON, THOMAS, agent in Forres, Moray, for the British Linen Company in 1849. [POD]

DAVIDSON, WILLIAM, born 1792, a seaman from Fraserburgh, aboard the Oscar of Aberdeen which, when bound for Greenland, was shipwrecked and drowned off Aberdeen on 1 April 1813. [Nigg gravestone, Aberdeenshire]

DAVIE, ALEXANDER, from Chapel of Garioch, Aberdeenshire, settled in Ashland County, Ohio, married Isobel Duffus from Insch, moved to Poweshiek County, Iowa, in 1866. [ENES.I.253]

DEAN, JOHN, from Moray, graduated MA from King's College, Aberdeen, in March 1828. [KCA]

DEASON, GEORGE, from Banff, graduated MA from King's College, Aberdeen, on 27 March 1795. [KCA]

DEMPSTER, JAMES, from Banff, graduated MA from King's College, Aberdeen, in March 1828, later a schoolmaster in Rothes. [KCA]

DEMPSTER, ROBERT, a merchant in Nairn, was accused of assault in Deer, Aberdeenshire, died in 1817. [NRS.AD14.17.69]

DEWARS, Mr, a teacher in Banff in 1836. [AOB.ii.207]

DEY, ROBERT, from Dufftown, Banffshire, married Charlotte Sarah Cameron, second daughter of D. Cameron from Inverness-shire, in New York on 3 April 1873. [EC.27629]

DIACK, ISABELLA, daughter of Alexander Diack a farmer in Mastrick, Rayne, Aberdeenshire, married George Smith of the Caledonian Hotel in Dunedin, Otago, New Zealand, on 6 June 1862. [AJ.5982]

DICK, PETER, son of John Dick a farmer on Laighmoor, Kennethmont, Aberdeenshire, died in New York on 24 April 1855. [AJ.5.12.1855]

DICKIE, GEORGE, born 1804, son of George Dickie a farmer in Auchmonziel, New Deer, Aberdeenshire, died in Hotitikia, New Zealand, on 28 July 1867. [AJ.6258]

DICKSON, GEORGE, agent in Grantown on Spey fr the Caledonian Banking Company in 1849. [POD]

DICKSON, WILLIAM, son of Adam Dickson in Fyvie, Aberdeenshire, a student in Marischal College in 1790s. [MCA]

DINGWALL, ARTHUR FORDYCE, baptised 26 August 1789, son of Reverend William Dingwall in Forgue, Aberdeenshire, a soldier from 1806 until his death at Muttra, India on 16 December 1830, Captain of the 19th Native Infantry of the Bengal Army. [BA.2.64]

DINGWALL, Mrs ELIZABETH, widow of Arthur Dingwall of Renneston, Aberdeenshire, late merchant in St John, New Brunswick, died in St John, N.B., on 25 March 1820. [CG.29.3.1820]

DINGWALL-FORDYCE, ARTHUR, baptised on 12 July 1783, son of Arthur Dingwall-Fordyce of Culsh and his wife Janet Morrison, a soldier from 1797 to his death at sea on 22 December 1812, Chief Engineer in Penang. [BA.2.204]

DIVORTY, ANDREW, second son of Andrew Divorty a bookseller in Elgin, Moray, died in Sydney, New South Wales, Australia, on 24 April 1856. [AJ.5667]

DIVORTY, GEORGE, son of James Divorty a farmer in Kintore, Aberdeenshire, was educated at Marischal College, Aberdeen, in 1846, later a minister in Australia. [MCA]

DONALD, ALEXANDER, from Banff, graduated MA from King's College, Aberdeen, on 29 March 1792. [KCA]

DONALD, ROBERT, a shipmaster in Stonehaven, Kincardineshire, testament, 1811, Comm. St Andrews. [NRS]

DONALD, THOMAS, from Banff, graduated MA from King's College, Aberdeen, on 30 March 1790. [KCA]

DONALD, WILLIAM, son of John Donald a carpenter in Grange, graduated MA from Marischal College in 1828, later a Presbyterian minister in New Brunswick, Canada. [MCA]

DONALDSON, ELIZABETH, daughter of William Donaldson, married William Innes from Demerara, in Elgin, Moray in July 1801. [GC.1547]

DONALDSON, ISABELLA, born 1720, died 1 January 1798, widow of Captain Charles Forbes of the 60th Regiment of Foot who was killed at Ticonderoga, New York, in 1758. [Banff gravestone]

DOUGAL, ALEXANDER, born 21 January 1782 in Forres, Moray, son of Dr Hugh Dougal and his wife Jean Seaton, a Lieutenant of the 1st Native Infantry Regiment of the Bengal Army from 1798 until his death at Midnapore, India, on 18 December 1802. [BA.2.70]

DOWN, HELEN, widow of Donald Mckay a labourer in Newlands of Kilravock, Nairn, was accused of stealing sheep in 1825. [NRS.AD14.25.229]

DOWNIE, ELSPETH, wife of Alexander Watt a packet fisher in Broadsea, Fraserburgh, Aberdeenshire, was accused of mobbing and rioting there in 1813. [NRS.AD4.13.88]

DRUM, ALEXANDER, a seaman in Gardenstown, later in Portsoy, testament, 1812, Comm. Aberdeen. [NRS]

DUFF, ALEXANDER, born 1771, son of Reverend Duff in Foveran, Aberdeenshire, died in Amhersburg, Upper Canada, on 10 June 1809. [SM.71.799]

DUFF, ARTHUR, son of Patrick Duff the town clerk of Elgin, Moray, a student at Marischal College from 1813 to 1817, later Sheriff Clerk of Elgin. [MCA]

DUFF, JAMES, born 1741, late in Madeira, was admitted as a burgess of Banff in 1779, [BBR], died on 1 April 1812. [Banff gravestone]

DUFF, JAMES, MP for Banffshire, [later Earl of Fife], was admitted as a burgess of Banff in 1837. [BBR]

DUFF, JOHN, a Lieutenant Colonel on Honourable East India Company Service, was admitted as a burgess of Banff in 1813. [BBR]

DUFF, PATRICK, born 1742, son of James Duff of Pitchaish, a soldier from 1760 until 1797, a Major General of the Bengal Army in India, died in Edinburgh on 2 February 1803. [BA.2.91]

DUFF, ROBERT, from Banff, graduated MA from King's College, Aberdeen, in March 1828, later minister at All Saints in Berbice. [KCA]

DUFF, WILLIAM, born 1754, Major of the 26th Regiment, died 1795. [Banff gravestone]

DUFF, WILLIAM, son of James Duff of Pitchaish, a soldier from 1777 until his death at Komona on 18 November 1807, a Lieutenant Colonel of the 9th Native Infantry Regiment of the Bengal Army. [BA.2.92]

DUFF, WILLIAM, settled in St George, Grenada, was admitted as a burgess of Banff in 1797. [BBR]

DUFF, WILLIAM, from Banff, graduated MA from King's College, Aberdeen, on 31 March 1810, later in the Service of the East India Company. [KCA]

DUFF, WILLIAM LATIMER, born 12 October 1822, son of Reverend William Duff and his wife Mary Steinson in Grange of Strathbogie, Aberdeenshire, a General of the United States Army, died on 27 June 1894. [F.6.315]

DUFFUS, ALEXANDER, born 1783 in Moray, a merchant who was naturalised in Charleston, South Carolina, on 15 November 1805. [NARA.M1183.1]

DUFFUS, ALEXANDER, a farmer from Insch, Aberdeenshire, emigrated with his wife and family to Poweshiek County, Iowa, in 1854. [ENES.1.253]

DUFFUS, JAMES, a merchant in Elgin, Moray, was appointed as Collector of the Triple Assessment, on 2 April 1798. [Records of Elgin.i.507]

DUFFUS, JAMES, a farmer from Insch, Aberdeenshire, emigrated with his wife and family to Poweshiek County, Iowa, in 1854. [ENES.1.253]

DUFFUS, JOHN, born 19 August 1771 in Elgin, Moray, died 19 July 1840 in Charleston, South Carolina. [Old Scots gravestone, Charleston]

DUGUID, LESLIE, son of William Duguid a merchant in Aberdeen, was educated at Marischal College around 1820, later a banker in Sydney, New South Wales, Australia. [MCA]

DUGUID, MARGARET, widow of Andrew Henry a shipmaster in Peterhead, Aberdeenshire, testament, 1795, Comm. Aberdeen. [NRS]

DUNBAR, ALEXANDER, a merchant from Nairn, died in Kingston, Jamaica, on 18 April 1794. [SM.56.442][EA][GM.64.768]

DUNBAR, ARCHIBALD, a Writer to the Signet, in the Manse of Rathen, Aberdeenshire, testament, 1809, Comm. Aberdeen. [NRS]

DUNBAR, Misses, mistresses of the Banff Boarding and Day School in 1828. [AOB.ii.206]

DUNCAN, ALEXANDER, husband of Barbara Hay, in Collieston, Slains, Aberdeenshire, a member of the Aberdeenshire Militia in 1807. [ACA.AS.AMI.6.1.1]

DUNCAN, George, born 1812, died in Landsend Culvie on 22 November 1883, husband of Elsie Gray, born 1819, died 23 November 1874, their son George Duncan, born 1844, for 6 years was a missionary in China, died in Torquay, England, on 12 February 1873. [Marnoch gravestone, Banffshire]

DUNCAN, JAMES, from Elgin, Moray, settled in Charleston, South Carolina, naturalised there on 23 April 1839. [NARA.M1183]

DUNCAN, JOSEPH, from Cromar, Aberdeenshire, graduated MA from King's College, Aberdeen, on 28 March 1794, later minister at Kilrenny. [KCA]

DUNCAN, THOMAS, born 2 September 1828 near Foveran, Aberdeenshire, son of George Duncan and his wife Elspet Webster, married Margaret Smart on 1 May 1858, emigrated to America in 1860, a textile manufacturer in Philadelphia, Pennsylvania, died there on 19 January 1887. [AP]

DUNN, WILLIAM, born 1782, a seaman from Raffan, Aberdeenshire, aboard the whaling ship Oscar of Aberdeen, when bound for Greenland, was shipwrecked and drowned off Aberdeen on 1 April 1813. [AJ]

DUNN, WILLIAM R., born 1857 in Huntly, Aberdeenshire, died in Georgetown, Demerara, on 2 July 1884. [AJ.29.7.1884]

DURNO, JAMES, a watchmaker, son of James Durno in New Deer, Aberdeenshire, died in Philadelphia, Pennsylvania, on 2 May 1835. [AJ.4575]

DURWARD, JAMES, from Aboyne, Aberdeenshire, graduated MA from King's College, Aberdeen, on 30 March 1791. [KCA]

DURWARD, JOSEPH, at Drumnyochar, Arbuthnott, Kincardineshire, testament, 1797, Comm. St Andrews. [NRS]

DUTHIE, ROBERT, a white-fisher in Inverallochy, Rathen, Aberdeenshire, testament, 1806. [NRS.CC1]

DUTHIE, WILLIAM, a white-fisher in Inverallochy, Rathen, Aberdeenshire, testament, 1806. [NRS.CC1]

DUTHIE, WILLIAM, master of the Eliza of Peterhead, Aberdeenshire, trading between Riga, Latvia, and Inverness in 1807. [NRS.E504.17.8]

DUTHIE, WILLIAM, husband of Christine Robertson in Peterhead, Aberdeenshire, was a member of the Aberdeenshire Miitia in 1808. [ACA.AS.AMI.6.1.1]

DYCE, ROBERT, son of Alexander Dyce of Tillygreig, Udny, Aberdeenshire, a student at Marischal College around 1817, later an Advocate in Aberdeen. [MCA]

EASTON, CHRISTINA, daughter of James Easton in Foveran, Aberdeenshire, wife of George Rennie, died in Otago, New Zealand, on 9 September 1869. [AJ.6361]

ELDER, ADAM, born 1747, died 21 June 1829, husband of Ann …., born 1752, died 25 April 1821. [Banff gravestone]

ELLIS, JAMES, miller at the Mill of Chapeltoun, testament, 1792, Comm. Aberdeen. [NRS]

ELLIS, WILLIAM, in Banff, testament, 1794, Comm. Aberdeen. [NRS]

ELMSLIE, ALEXANDER, son of Gavin Elmslie in Bourtrie, a student at Marischal College in 1830s, later in Australia. [MCA]

ELMSLIE, ALEXANDER LEITH, in Banff, graduated MD from King's College, Aberdeen, on 9 October 1840. [KCA]

ELMSLIE, GEORGE, born 1835, son of George Elmslie at Foot o'Hill, Gartly, Aberdeenshire, died at his brother's house in Brooklyn, New York, on 16 December 1875. [AJ.22.12.1875]

ELMSLIE, PETER, in Huntly, Aberdeenshire, father of Elizabeth McCombie Elmslie, born 1853, wife of Francis Leys, died in Buenos Ayres, Argentina, on 12 July 1878. [EC.29293]

ELMSLIE, WILLIAM WALKER, from Aberdeenshire, married Harriet Ann Kennedy, daughter of William Kennedy of St John, New Brunswick, there on 7 March 1822. [CG.13.3.1822]

ELRICK, ALEXANDER, sometime in Wester Craigie, Belhelvie, Aberdeenshire, testament, 1791, Comm. Aberdeen. [NRS]

ESSON, HELEN, youngest daughter of Robert Esson in Balnacraig, Aboyne, Aberdeenshire, married William Brass from Invercargill, New Zealand, in Dunedin, N.Z., on 24 June 1862. [AJ.5986]

ESSON, MARY, daughter of Robert Esson in Balnacraig, Aboyne, Aberdeenshire, married Robert Murray from Tokomairo, New Zealand, in Dunedin, N.Z., on 24 June 1862. [AJ.5986]

FAIRBAIRN, FRANCIS, born 23 August 1770, son of James Fairbairn in Tarland, Aberdeenshire, a grocer in New York, died in Belleville, New York, on 29 October 1830. [ANY.I.366]

FALCONER, ALEXANDER, son of William Falconer in Kinerniry, Banffshire, a writer in Elgin, Moray, was admitted as a Notary Public on 7 July 1791. [NRS.NP2.34.281]

FALCONER, ALEXANDER, from Banff, graduated MA from King's College, Aberdeen, on 28 March 1799. [KCA]

FALCONER, ALEXANDER, a shipmaster in Garmouth, Moray, a sasine, 1808. [NRS.RS.Elgin.716]

FALCONER, ARCHIBALD, tenant in Milton of Kilravock, Nairnshire, testament, 1791 Comm. Aberdeen. [NRS]

FALCONER, JAMES, a purser in the Royal Navy residing in Stonehaven, Kincardineshire, later in Aberdeen, testament 1791, Comm. Aberdeen. [NRS]

FALCONER, JAMES, a landsman aboard HMS Trusty, husband of Mrs Lily Falconer in Bervie, Kincardineshire, 1797. [TRA.CE70.1.8/6]

FALCONER, JAMES, born 1724, a seaman in Stonehaven, Kincardineshire, died 9 September 1804. [Cowie gravestone]

FALCONER, JOHN, from Nairn, graduated MA from King's College, Aberdeen, in March 1834, later a minister at Newbyth. [KCA]

FALCONER, PATRICK, born 1775, son of William Falconer, [1720-1793], a farmer at Kinnermony, and his wife Anna Rose, [1743-1821], settled in New York in 1794, a merchant at 13 Broadway, N.Y., died in 1837. [Inveravon gravestone, Banffshire][ANY][1812]

FALCONER, ROBERT, born 1782, son of William Falconer, [1720-1793], a farmer in Kinnermony, and his wife Anna Rose, [1743-1821], a merchant in New York, died in 1851. [Inveravon gravestone, Banffshire]

FALCONER, WILLIAM, a wheelwright in Old Deer, Aberdeenshire, testament, 1792, Comm. Aberdeen. [NRS]

FALCONER, WILLIAM, born 1763, son of William Falconer, [1720-1793], and his wife Anna Rose, [1743-1821], a merchant in New York, died in 1837. [Inveravon gravestone, Banffshire]

FALCONER, WILLIAM, a wheelwright in Old Deer, Aberdeenshire, testament, 1792, Comm. Aberdeen. [NRS]

FALCONER, WILLIAM, a sailor in Peterhead, Aberdeenshire, father of Nathaniel Falconer a shipmaster in London, a sasine, 1792. [NRS.RS.Aberdeen.1048]

FARQUHAR, ALEXANDER, farmer in Aucheoch, testament, 1792, Comm. Aberdeen. [NRS]

FARQUHAR, ALEXANDER, born 1805, died 8 February 1891, husband of Mary ...., born 1805, died 7 April 1885. [Aboyne gravestone, Aberdeenshire]

FARQUHAR, ANDREW, eldest son of Andrew Farquhar in the Mains of Caskiben, died in St Thomas in the East, Jamaica, on 2 October 1834. .

FARQUHAR, HELEN, spouse of Andrew Riddell in Broomhills, testament, 1792, Comm. Aberdeen. [NRS]

FARQUHAR, JAMES, of Tullos, father of Robert Farquhar, a Lieutenant in the Service of the Honourable East India Company, 1832. [NRS.S/H]

FARQUHAR, THOMAS, in Aberdeenshire, graduated MD from King's College, Aberdeen, on 30 July 1846. [KCA]

FARQUHARSON, ALEXANDER, of Balfour, testament, 1792, Comm. Aberdeen. [NRS]

FARQUHARSON, ARCHIBALD, of Finzean, testament, 1798, Comm. Aberdeen. [NRS]

FARQUHARSON, DONALD, postmaster in Ballater, Aberdeenshire, died 20 December 1852, father of Robert Farquharson a physician in Berlin, Germany, 1868. [NRS.S/H]

FARQUHARSON, JAMES, agent of the North of Scotland Bank in Auchenblae, Kincardineshire, in 1849. [POD]

FARQUHARSON, JOHN, son of James Farquharson of Coldrach, died in Jamaica on 14 October 1808. [SM.11.237]

FARQUHARSON, MARY, in Fraserburgh, Aberdeenshire, testament, 1792, Comm. Aberdeen. [NRS]

FARQUHARSON, OCTAVIUS FREDERICK, born 16 January 1845, eighth son of James Farquharson of Invercauld, Aberdeenshire, died in Toolburra, Warwick, Queensland, Australia, on 16 September 1867. [AJ.6255][Braemar gravestone, Aberdeenshire]

FARQUHARSON, ROBERT DUNDAS ROSS, born 29 March 1840, fifth son of James Farquharson of Invercauld, Aberdeenshire, died in Cardwell, Queensland, Australia, on 18 January 1867. [AJ.6228][Braemar gravestone, Aberdeenshire]

FAYE, AMOUND, of Norway, was admitted as a burgess of Banff in 1785. [BBR]

FERGUSON, Captain WILLIAM, of the Artillery Company of the Peterhead Company of Volunteers, Aberdeenshire, letters, 1798-1801. [NRS.GD44.47.45.4]

FERRIER, JOHN, a ships carpenter in Banff, later in Aberdeen, testament, 1794, Comm. Aberdeen. [NRS]

FERRIER, WILLIAM, in High Street, Banff, applied to settle in Canada in June 1827. [TNA.CO384.5.847]

FETTES, ALEXANDER, born 18 March 1845 in Laurencekirk, died in South Africa on 24 March 1921. [St George gravestone, Port Elizabeth, Cape of Good Hope.]

FIDDES, ALEXANDER, from Banff, graduated MA from King's College, Aberdeen, on 28 March 1794. [KCA]

FINDLATOR, GEORGE, a cooper in Fraserburgh, Aberdeenshire, and Rebecca Durham, were married in Fraserburgh on 23 February 1800. [Fraserburgh Episcopalian Records]

FINDLATOR, JOHN, born 1747, a shoemaker in Macduff, Banffshire, died 6 June 1815. [Banff gravestone]

FINDLATOR, WILLIAM, a mariner from Stonehaven, Kincardineshire, was naturalised in Charleston, South Carolina, on 13 November 1796. [NARA.M1183.1]

FINDLAY, Mrs ELSPET, born 1796 in Moray, wife of James Findlay, died in Halifax, Nova Scotia, on 6 March 1835. [AR.7.3.1835]

FINDLAY, JAMES, a fisherman in Banff, then in the Seatown of Cullen, was ordered to be apprehended for not fulfilling a contract, in 1812. [Annals of Banff.i.351]

FINLAY, Reverend GEORGE, from Cullen, Banffshire, a Wesleyan missionary, emigrated in 1845, died at Cape Coast Castle, Ghana, on 10 March 1846. [AJ.5133]

FINLAY, JAMES, and Elspeth Shearer, both from Rothes, Moray, were married in Halifax, Nova Scotia, on 26 April 1825. [AR.30.4.1825]

FINDLAY, JAMES, from Moray, married Mrs Margaret Ann Gray of Halifax, Nova Scotia, there on 10 March 1836. [AR.12.3.1836]

FINDLAY, WILLIAM, born 1766 in Rothes, Moray, died in Halifax, Nova Scotia, on 4 August 1842. [Acadian Recorder.6.8.1842]

FINNIE, JOHN, a skipper in Macduff, testament, 1823, Comm. Aberdeen. [NRS]

FLETCHER, ALEXANDER, from the Mearns, [Kincardineshire], graduated MA from King's College, Aberdeen, on 27 March 1795. [KCA]

FLYTER, ALEXANDER, from Moray, graduated MA from King's College, Aberdeen, on 29 March 1805, later a schoolmaster in Fearn, then a Free Church minister in Rothesay and in Alness. [KCA]

FORBES, ALEXANDER, in the Mill of Fowles, testament, 1800, Comm. Aberdeen. [NRS]

FORBES, ALEXANDER, born 1783 in Peterhead, Aberdeenshire, a merchant who was naturalised in South Carolina on 14 December 1807. [NARA.M1183.1]

FORBES, ALEXANDER, a white-fisher in Torry, Nigg, Kincardine, testament, 1820, Comm. St Andrews. [NRS]

FORBES, ANDREW, son of George Forbes of Upper Boyndlie, Banffshire, a writer in Edinburgh, was admitted as a Notary Public on 6 December 1791. [NRS.NP2.34.301]

FORBES, ANDREW, a white-fisher in Torry, Nigg, Kincardine, testament, 1816, Comm. St Andrews. [NRS]

FORBES, ANDREW, a purser in the Royal Navy, later in Peterhead, testament, 1819, Comm. Aberdeen. [NRS]

FORBES, ARTHUR, born 1757, farmer at Drumgesk, died on 31 December 1841, husband of Elizabeth Smith, born 1771, died in Cockenzie on 10 September 1855. [Aboyne gravestone, Aberdeenshire]

FORBES, CHARLES, of Auchernack, testament, 1793, Comm. Aberdeen. [NRS]

FORBES, CHARLES, of Auchmeddan, MP, was admitted as a burgess of Banff in 1813. [BBR]

FORBES, DAVID, minister at Laurencekirk, Kincardineshire, testament, 1800, Comm. St Andrews. [NRS]

FORBES, DAVID, born in New Mills, Banffshire, died in New York on 8 March 1856. [AJ.9.4.1856]

FORBES, ELIZABETH, daughter of Captain John Forbes of Boyndlie, sometime spouse of bailie George Philip a merchant in Banff, later spouse to James Mackie of Gask, residing in Peterhead, Aberdeenshire, testament, 1799, Comm. Aberdeen. [NRS]

FORBES, FRANCIS, from Aberdeenshire, graduated MA from King's College, Aberdeen, in 1821, minister of St Luke's, British Guiana. [KCA]

FORBES, GEORGE, son of George Forbes in Aberdeenshire, a student in Marischal College in 1790s. [MCA]

FORBES, GEORGE, of Upper Boyndlie, Aberdeenshire, testament, 1794, Comm. Aberdeen. [NRS]

FORBES, GEORGE, son of Captain I. Forbes in Glenconry, died in Bombay, India, in 1804. [AJ]

FORBES, GEORGE, from Kinord, a master in the Royal Navy, testament, 1821, Comm. Aberdeen. [NRS]

FORBES, JAMES, in New York, heir to his aunt Euphame Forbes, widow of George Strachan Kitj of Auchorsk, in 1825. [NRS.S/H]

FORBES, JAMES, from Boyndie, Banffshire, a merchant in Bombay, India, in 1839. [NRS.S/H]

FORBES, JOHN, son of George Forbes of Lockermick, a soldier from 1765 until 1803, Major General of the Bengal Army, died in Dunbar on 2 October 1808. [BA.2.200]

FORBES, JOHN, of Skellatur, born 1732, Governor of Rio de Janeiro, died there on 8 April 1808. [AJ]

FORBES, JOHN, born in Gamrie, Banffshire, on 20 December 1767, son of James Forbes and his wife Sarah Gordon, a merchant in Florida and the Bahamas, probate 2 October 1820 in Mobile. [Will Book i]

FORBES, JOHN, of New, a benefactor of King's College, Aberdeen, on 2 May 1820. [KCA]

FORBES, JOHN MURRAY, a minister at St Luke's, New York, heir to his grand-aunt Margaret Forbes or Paterson in New Mill, Keith, Banffshire, 1836. [NRS.S/H]

FORBES, LEWIS ALEXANDER, born 10 March 1823 in Boharm, Banffshire, son of Reverend Lewis Alexander Forbes and his wife Penelope Cowie, died in Geelong, New South Wales on 30 April 1852. [F.6.338]

FORBES, ROBERT, son of Reverend Robert Forbes in Monymusk, Aberdeenshire, was educated at Marischal College in the 1820s, later a Proctor in Colombo, Ceylon. [MCA]

FORBES, WILLIAM NAIRN, born 3 April 1796 in Auchterless, Aberdeenshire, son of John Forbes of Blackford and his wife Anne Margaret Gregory, a soldier from 1815 to his death at sea on 1 May 1855, a Major General of the Bengal Army. [BA]

FORBES, WILLIAM, a merchant in Peterhead, Aberdeenshire, a sequestration book 1818-1821. [NRS.CS96.680.1/2]

FORBES-LEITH, RALPH, MD, son of George Forbes-Leith of Knock, died in Carriacou, Grenada, on 22 August 1868. [AJ.4.11.1868]

FORBES-LEITH, THEODORE GEORGE, born 7 October 1813, son of George Forbes-Leith of Knock, an Ensign of the Bengal Army from 1832 until his death at Arakan on 16 July 1839. [BA.2.202]

FORD, HENRY, from Nairn, a surgeon in the Royal Navy, testament, 1808, Comm. Moray. [NRS]

FORDYCE, WILLIAM DINGWALL, a writer in Aberdeen, son of Arthur Dingwall Fordyce the commissary of Aberdeenshire, was admitted as a Notary Public on 17 January 1794, died 1 March 1831. [NRS.NP2.35.103]

FORDYCE, WILLIAM, second son of William Dingwall of Techmuiry and his wife Margaret Ritchie, died in Charleston, South Carolina, on 13 April 1839. [St Nicholas gravestone, Aberdeen]

FORREST, DAVID, son of James Forrest a merchant in Drumlithie, Kincardineshire, graduated MA from Marischal College in 1819, later a surgeon in the Service of the East India Company. [MCA]

FORREST, GEORGE, from Auchneive, Tarves, Aberdeenshire, drowned on his passage from New York to Glasgow in 1869. [AJ.7.7.1869]

FORREST, JAMES, born 25 October 1764, son of William Forrest in Cruden, Aberdeenshire, a bank accountant in USA, died on 20 September 1831. [ANY]

FORSYTH, ALEXANDER, son of John Forsyth a merchant in Elgin, Moray, was apprenticed to George Sim a saddler in Aberdeen in 1790. [ACA]

FORSYTH, ALEXANDER, a writer in Edinburgh, son of John Forsyth a wright in Cullen, Banffshire, was admitted as a Notary Public on 9 March 1799. [NRS.NP2.36.259]

FORSYTH, JOHN ALEXANDER, born 25 February 1770, son of Reverend William Forsyth and his wife Margaret Turner in Aboyne, Aberdeenshire, died in Jamaica on 20 February 1800. [F.6.78]

FORSYTH, JOHN, born 19 September 1784, son of John Forsyth in Newhills, Aberdeenshire, settled in Newburgh, New York, married Jane Currie on 11 January 1810. [American Armory and Blue Book]

FORSYTH, JOHN, son of Robert Forsyth from Huntly, Aberdeenshire, a student at Marischal College around 1819, later a surgeon in the Royal Navy. [MCA]

FORSYTH, JOSEPH, born 1760 in Huntly, Aberdeenshire, son of William Forsyth and his wife Jean Phyn, emigrated to Canada before 1797, a merchant who died on 20 September 1813. [DCB]

FORSYTH, WILLIAM, a farmer in Duffus, Moray, was shipping consignments of grain via the harbour of Burghead in 1790s. [Records of Elgin.i.502]

FORSYTH, WILLIAM, in New Providence, in the Bahamas, died in 1797, youngest son of James Forsyth, a farmer in Old Duffus, Elgin, Moray, and his wife Isobel Naughty, testament, 1810, Comm. Edinburgh. [NRS]

FORSYTH, WILLIAM, from Huntly, Aberdeenshire, died in Trinidad on 4 January 1851. [AJ.5374]

FOWLER, ALEXANDER, born 1786, gamekeeper at Dunlugas, died in Banff on 10 July 1835. [Banff gravestone]

FOWLER, JOHN, master of the Hope of Nairn trading between Ballachulish and Inverness in 1813. [NRS.E504.17.8]

FRASER, ALEXANDER, of Strichen, Aberdeenshire, a Senator of the College of Justice, testament, 1792, Comm. Aberdeen. [NRS]

FRASER, ALEXANDER, a shipmaster in Peterhead, Aberdeenshire, testament, 1796, Comm. Aberdeen. [NRS]

FRASER, FRANCIS, of Findrack, the elder, testament, 1792, Comm. Aberdeen. [NRS]

FRASER, HUGH, born 1769 in Moray, Professor of Divinity in Georgetown, South Carolina, was naturalised in Charleston, S.C., on 21 February 1817. [NARA.M1183.1]

FRASER, JAMES, of Fingask, died in St Kitts in 1813. [EA.5173.13]

FRASER, JAMES, born 1769. In Aberdeenshire, died in Halifax, Nova Scotia, on 15 July 1839. [AR.20.7.1839]

FRASER, JAMES, born 1817, in Nairnside, Daviot, died 18 February 1885, husband of Helen Cameron, born 1816, died 21 April 1872, parents of Kenneth Fraser, born 1845, died in Australia on 16 December 1877. [Daviot gravestone]

FRASER, JAMES, an elder of the parish of Banff in 1834. [AOB.ii.116]

FRASER, JAMES, from Forres, Moray, graduated MA from King's College, Aberdeen, in March 1834, later minister at Colvend. [KCA]

FRASER, JOHN, in Wester Micras, Aberdeenshire, testament, 1791, Comm. Aberdeen. [NRS]

FRASER, PETER, born 1766 in Forres, Moray, died in Fredericton, New Brunswick, on 13 August 1840, [NBC.22.8.1840]

FRASER, ROBERT W., MA, in Huntly, Aberdeenshire, graduated MD from King's College, Aberdeen, on 29 April 1841. [KCA]

FRASER, THOMAS, in Tolmaads, testament, 1798, Comm. Aberdeen. [NRS]

FRASER, THOMAS, a skipper in Peterhead, Aberdeenshire, testament, 1816, Comm. Aberdeen. [NRS]

FRASER, WILLIAM, Captain of the Fraserburgh Volunteers, Aberdeenshire, letters, 1798-1807. [NRS.GD44.47.2-3]

FRASER, WILLIAM, born 22 December 1763, second son of Francis Fraser of Findrack, Aberdeenshire, was educated in Aberdeen and in Cambridge, Rector of Trelawney parish, Jamaica, died in Falmouth, Jamaica, on 1 April 1844. [Falmouth gravestone]

FRASER, WILLIAM, in Huntly, Aberdeenshire, formerly a farmer in Canada, brother of John Fraser a merchant in Huntly, who died on 24 May 1863. [NRS.S/H]

FRASER, Captain, master of the Lion of Aberdeen from Peterhead, Aberdeenshire, to Savannah, Georgia, in 1856. [AJ]

FREEMAN, ALEXANDER, born 1711, a seaman in Skateraw, Kincardineshire, died 22 February 1793. [Cowie gravestone]

FRENCH, Mrs ELIZABETH, second daughter of William Ross in Huntly, Aberdeenshire, married Alexander Sutherland, from St Kilda, Inverness, in Melbourne, Victoria, Australia, on 19 August 1856. [AJ.5681]

FYFE, ALEXANDER, a merchant in Nairn, sederunt book, 1826-1827. [NRS.CS96.840]

FYFE, MACDUFF, son of John Fyfe in the Cabrach, Banffshire, graduated MA from Marischal College, Aberdeen, in 1789, a planter on St Vincent. [MCA]

GADIE, WILLIAM, a skipper in Peterhead, Aberdeenshire, inventory, 1823, Comm. Aberdeen. [NRS]

GAIRDEN, GEORGE, son of George Gairden a merchant in Banff, died in Jamaica on 30 October 1792. [SM.55.50]

GALE, ALEXANDER, born 18 December 1800, son of John Gale a farmer in Coldstone, Aberdeenshire, and his wife Jean Esson, was educated at Marischal College, graduated MA there in 1819, later a Presbyterian minister in Hamilton, Ontario. [KCA][MCA]

GALL, JOHN, born 22 December 1830 in Dallfour, Glen Muick, Aberdeenshire, died at Ballater House, Kingston, South Australia, on 10 December 1907. [Glencairn gravestone, Dumfries-shire]

GALL, WILLIAM, agent of the Aberdeen Bank in Banff in 1849. [POD]

GALLAIRD, JOHN, of Charleston, South Carolina, was admitted as a burgess of Banff in 1785. [BBR] [TNA.AO.12.73.137]

GALLAIRD, SAMUEL, of Charleston, South Carolina, was admitted as a burgess of Banff in 1785. [BBR]

GALLAIRD, THEODORE, of Charleston, South Carolina, was admitted as a burgess of Banff in 1785. [BBR][TNA.AO.12.92.1A]

GALLOWAY, GEORGE, son of James Galloway a shoemaker in Peterhead, graduated MA from Marischal College in 1833, later a Presbyterian minister in Toronto, Canada. [MCA]

GAMMACK, ALEXANDER, son of William Gammack a lawyer in Peterhead, graduated MA in 1854, and MD in 1856 from Marischal College, later surgeon major of the Indian Medical Service. [MCA]

GAMMACK, JACOBINA, born 1786, midwife in Aberchirder, died 5 August 1870. [Marnoch gravestone, Banffshire]

GAMMACK, JAMES, born 1797, a watchmaker who died in Canada on 23 December 1859. [Marnoch gravestone, Banffshire]

GAMMACK, JAMES, son of Alexander Gammack in Turriff, Aberdeenshire, graduated MA from Marischal College in 1857, later an Episcopal minister in West Hartford, USA. [MCA]

GAMMACK, JOHN HUTCHISON, son of William Gammack a solicitor in Peterhead, graduated MA from Marischal College in 1856, later manager of an agricultural company in Newcastle, New South Wales, Australia. [MCA]

GAMMIE, WILLIAM, born 1744, farmer at Knight's Mill, died 23 September 1821, husband of Isobel Troup, born 1767, died 11 July 1827. [Marnoch gravestone, Banffshire]

GARDEN, Dr ALEXANDER, late in Charleston, South Carolina, died in London on 15 April 1791. [GM.61.389] [TNA.AO.12.50.146]

GARDEN, ALEXANDER, of Troup, Banffshire, testament, 1792, Comm. Aberdeen. [NRS]

GARDEN, FRANCIS, the younger of Troup, was admitted as a burgess of Banff in 1811. [BBR]

GARDEN, JOHN, at Gateside of Newpark, Newhills, Aberdeenshire, testament, 1797, Comm. Aberdeen. [NRS]

GARDINER, GEORGE, a shoemaker, was ordained as an elder in Banff on 21 March 1841. [AOB.ii.122]

GARDINER, JAMES, born 1760, son of James Gardiner born 1720, died 22 April 1790, and his wife Elspet Wilson born 1700, died 1795, late in Jamaica, thereafter in Banff, died 8 May 1831, testament, 30 October 1820. [NRS.Aberdeen.W993]; husband of Margaret Aven. [Banff gravestone]

GARDINER, JAMES, late in Jamaica, died in Banff on 22 May 1820. [SM.86.96]

GARDINER, WILLIAM, son of John Gardiner a farmer in Smithston, Aberdeenshire, a writer in Aberdeen, was admitted as a Notary Public on 13 June 1791, an advocate in Aberdeen in 1793, died on 5 November 1826. [NRS.NP2.34.267]

GARIOCH, ALEXANDER, a shipmaster in Peterhead, Aberdeenshire, a sasine, 1794. [NRS.RS.Aberdeen.1292]

GARROW, MARY, daughter of John Garrow a manufacturer, and widow of Alexander Barclay late of Elgin Academy, Moray, married John Anderson of Miramachi, New Brunswick, in Aberdeen on 22 September 1831. [AR.3.9.1831] [AJ]

GATHERER, JOHN, a writer in Edinburgh, son of John Gatherer a farmer in Elgin, Moray, was admitted as a Notary Public on 21 January 1795. [NRS.NP2.35.221]

GAULD, HUGH, a coppersmith in Fraserburgh, Aberdeenshire, was accused of mobbing and rioting there in 1813. [NRS.AD4.13.88]

GAULD, JOHN, from Coldstone, Aberdeenshire, graduated MA from King's College, Aberdeen, in March 1844, later a Free Church minister in Canada. [KCA]

GAVIN, RICHARD, son of Dr William Gavin in Strichen, Aberdeenshire, graduated MA from Marischal College in 1839, later a minister in Canada. [MCA]

GAVIN, WILLIAM, in Drumlithie, Kincardineshire, brother and heir of John Gavin in Grenada, 1832. [NRS.S/H]

GEDDES, CHRISTINA, born 1821, wife of James Hynd a merchant in Huntly, Aberdeenshire, died 14 December 1853. [Ruthven gravestone]

GEDDES, JAMES, a solicitor in Canada West, grandson and heir of James Geddes a flax-dresser in Gardenstown, Banffshire, who died in 1786. [NRS.S/H]

GEDDES, JAMES, a civil engineer in Nashville, Tennessee, grandson and heir of Alexander Geddes in Portsoy, Banffshire, who died 27 March 1810. [NRS.S/H]

GEDDES, PETER, a snuff manufacturer in Banff, was admitted as a burgess of Banff in 1823. [BBR]

GEDDES, PETER, born 1800, a painter in Banff, died 24 November 1848. [Banff gravestone]

GEDDES, WILLIAM, HEICS, from Fochabers, Moray, graduated MD from King's College, Aberdeen, on 11 June 1843. [KCA]

GEDDIE, THOMAS, born 1740, a cooper in Banff, died 19 October 1819, husband of Ann Ross, born 1745, died 30 September 1815. [Banff gravestone]

GENTLE, ALEXANDER, minister of Alves, Moray, married Isabella Bogle, daughter of Lauchlan Bogle in Jamaica, at 27 Castle Street, Edinburgh, on 23 October 1828. [S.918.689]

GEORGE, JOHN, a farmer in Cowdenknowes, was ordained as an elder in Banff on 21 March 1841. [AOB.ii.122]

GEORGE, PETER, from Banff, graduated MA from King's College, Aberdeen, on 27 March 1800. [KCA]

GERRARD, ANDREW, born 1797, in New Aberdour, died 28 June 1890, husband of Margaret Laird, born 1808, died 15 March 1868. [Aberdour gravestone, Aberdeenshire]

GERARD, GEORGE, jr., of Midstrath, residing at Haughs of Ashogle, testament, 1799, Comm. Aberdeen. [NRS]

GIBBON, WILLIAM DUFF, son of Charles Gibbon a minister in Lonmay, Aberdeenshire, a student at Marischal College in the 1850s, later an estate agent in Kandy, Ceylon. [MCA]

GIBSON, ALEXANDER, son of William Gibson in Morphie, Ecclesgreig, Kincardineshire, a student at Marischal College around 1815, later a surgeon in the Service of the East India Company and Conservator of the forests in India. [MCA]

GIBSON, JAMES, in Seafield, eldest son of James Gibson in Upper Brogar, testament, 1791, Comm. Aberdeen. [NRS]

GIBSON, MARGARET, relict of George Courage in Belhelvie, and daughter of James Gibson in Upper Broggan, Slains, Aberdeenshire, testament, 1791, Comm. Aberdeen. [NRS]

GILCHRIST, Mrs MARGARET, in Peterhead, Aberdeenshire, relict of Harry Gilchrist a Lieutenant of the 42nd Regiment of Foot [the Black Watch], testament, 1796, Comm. Aberdeen. [NRS]

GILL, GEORGE, born 1809, died at North Essie, St Fergus, Aberdeenshire, on 29 January 1899, husband of Margaret Cumming, born 1824, died 23 February 1902. [Aberdour gravestone, Aberdeenshire.]

GILL, JAMES, a shipmaster in Portsoy, Banffshire, a sasine, 1795. [NRS.RS.Banff.414]

GILLANDERS, BARBARA, relict of Alexander Webster in Tarland Aberdeenshire, testament, 1797, Comm. Aberdeen. [NRS]

GILLESPIE, JOHN, gardener at Kittybrewster, Aberdeenshire, testament, 1798, Comm. Aberdeen. [NRS]

GILLICE, JOHN, son of John Gillice a writer in Keith, Banffshire, graduated MA from Marischal College in 1822, later a medical practitioner in America. [MCA]

GILMORE, ALEXANDER, from Oyne, Aberdeenshire, a farmer in Shag Valley, New Zealand, father of Margaret Ann Gilmore, who married William Diack, a farmer in Hillhead, Hawkesbury, N.Z., at the Caledonian Hotel, Dunedin, Otago, N.Z., on 25 July 1867. [AJ.6248]

GILZEAN, JOHN, a farmer, was admitted as a burgess of Elgin in 1796. [EBR]

GLEGG, Captain, master of the Lion of Aberdeen from Peterhead, Aberdeenshire, to Quebec in 1858. [AJ]

GLENNIE, ALEXANDER, formerly a merchant in New Deer, Aberdeenshire, died in Kyneston, Victoria, Australia, in February 1864. [AJ.6084]

GLENNIE, PATRICK, born 1844 in Ballater, Aberdeenshire, died in Thomastown, Connecticut, on 8 April 1873. [AJ.7.5.1873]

GODSMAN, ALEXANDER, born 1753 in Banffshire, died in Halifax, Nova Scotia, on 13 January 1819. [AR.16.1.1819]

GORDON, ALEXANDER, of Letterfourie, Aberdeen, testament, 1797, Comm. Aberdeen. [NRS]

GORDON, ALEXANDER, in Redmire, testament, 1800, Comm. Aberdeen. [NRS]

GORDON, ALEXANDER, a ship-builder in Peterhead, Aberdeenshire, versus James Macdonald, master of the Friendship of Inverness in 1834. [NRS.CS96.680.68]

GORDON, ANN, widow of Dr William Young, in Stonehaven, Kincardineshire, testament, 1796, Comm. St Andrews. [NRS]

GORDON, BERTHA, youngest daughter of Michael F. Gordon of Abergeldie, Aberdeenshire, married Charles Gordon MD, from Pernambuco, Brazil, in Gittesham, Devon, on 4 October 1855. [EEC.322801]

GORDON, CHARLES, of Abergeldie, Aberdeenshire, testaments, 1796-1797, Comm. Aberdeen. [NRS]

GORDON, CHARLES, son of James Gordon, in Ballater, Aberdeenshire, was educated at Marischal College in 1840s, graduated MD from

King's College, Aberdeen, on 26 July 1850, later in Brazil and Natal, South Africa. [KCA]

GORDON, CHARLES, of Woodside, father of John David Gordon a wine merchant in Xeres de la Frontera, Spain, 1834. [NRS.S/H]

GORDON, DAVID, son of John Gordon a farmer in Banff, a student at Marischal College in 1840s, later a Free Church minister in Montreal, Quebec. [MCA]

GORDON, DONALD, born 1784, a whisky smuggler and sometime horse dealer in Guernside, accused of forgery in 1830. [NRS.AD14.12]

GORDON, ELIZABETH, only child of John Gordon a shipmaster in Aberdeen, and spouse to Reverend George Mark in Peterculter, Aberdeenshire, testament, 1797, Comm. Aberdeen. [NRS]

GORDON, ELIZABETH, daughter of Charles Gordon of Buthlaw, testament, 1797, Comm. Aberdeen. [NRS]

GORDON, ELIZABETH SOPHIA, youngest daughter of William Gordon of Banff and of Dominica, married James Rae of the Royal Navy, in Chelsea, London, on 5 December 1827. [EA.6683.799]

GORDON, Mrs EMILY, wife of Hugh Gordon, died in Strathbogie, New England, New South Wales, Australia, on 19 November 1855. [AJ.5646]

GORDON, FRANCES, daughter of John Gordon of Baldornie, testament, 1792, Comm. Aberdeen. [NRS]

GORDON, FRANCIS, born 1782, from Huntly, Aberdeenshire, died in New York on 1 December 1862. [AJ.24.12.1862]

GORDON, GEORGE, in Edenton, North Carolina, brother and heir of Clementina Gordon in Cairnfield, Banff, 1847. [NRS.S/H]

GORDON, HANNAH, daughter of Francis Gordon in New York, late in Huntly, Aberdeenshire, died in St Kitts on 8 September 1862. [AJ.29.10.1862]

GORDON, HELEN, sometime spouse to James Innes, thereafter relict of James Alexander a wright in Banff, testament, 1798, Comm. Aberdeen. [NRS]

GORDON, JAMES, of Letterfowrie, testament, 1790, Comm. Aberdeen. [NRS]

GORDON, JAMES, son of George Gordon of Westfaulds of Glass, Aberdeenshire, a writer in Peterhead, Aberdeenshire, was admitted as a Notary Public on 6 February 1790, died 6 December 1806. [NRS.CC1.6.75.204300; NP2.34.145]

GORDON, JAMES, from Banff, graduated MA from King's College, Aberdeen, on 27 March 1800. [KCA]

GORDON, Captain JAMES, late of the Aberdeenshire Militia, died in Port Maria, Jamaica, on 20 November 1820. [BM.9.121]

GORDON, JAMES, a poacher in Ballater, Aberdeenshire, 1833-1835. [NRS.GD45.18.2362]

GORDON, JEAN, in Turriff, Aberdeenshire, was victim of an assault there in 1835. [NRS.AD14.35.70]

GORDON, JOHN, born 24 March 1782, son of Thomas Gordon in Aboyne, Aberdeenshire, was educated at King's College, Aberdeen, from 1795 to 1799, settled in Jamaica. [KCA]

GORDON, JOHN, son of John Gordon of Coharoie, was apprenticed to James Finnie a wright in Aberdeen, in 1791. [ACA]

GORDON, JOHN, in Whitehouse of Maryculter, Aberdeenshire, testament, 1792, Comm. Aberdeen. [NRS]

GORDON, JOHN, a salmon fisher at the Bridge of Don, Aberdeenshire, testament, 1793, Comm. Aberdeen. [NRS]

GORDON, JOHN, born 1797, blacksmith at Saphock, died 25 October 1875, husband of Rachel McKay, born 1806, died 1 April 1882. [Daviot gravestone]

GORDON, JOHN, of Murtle, a benefactor of King's College, Aberdeen, on 11 August 1815. [KCA]

GORDON, JOHN, of Delnabo, Moray, died at Blackwall, Richmond River, New South Wales, Australia, on 17 August 1855. [AJ.5641]

GORDON, JOHN DAVID, of Wardhouse and Kildrummy, Aberdeenshire, died on 20 May 1866, brother of Maria de la Conception in Madrid, Spain. [NRS.S/H]

GORDON, Lady Katherine, daughter of the Duke of Gordon, and wife of Captain Thomas Booker of the 53rd Regiment, testament, 1797, Comm. Aberdeen. [NRS]

GORDON, LEWIS, son of Alexander Gordon of Belnabodach, was apprenticed to John Gordon a merchant in Aberdeen in 1790. [ACA]

GORDON, MADELINA, fourth daughter of William Gordon of Aberdour, married John Murray McGusty, in Georgetown, Demerara, on 20 June 1825. [S.587.543]

GORDON, MAGDALENE, daughter of John Gordon of the Mortlach Distillery in Banffshire, married James Henry Rule, son of James Rule of Richmond, in Melbourne, Victoria, Australia, on 12 June 1856. [AJ.5671]

GORDON, Mrs MARY, widow of Alexander Gordon an Excise officer in Old Meldrum, Aberdeenshire, testament, 1791, Comm. Aberdeen. [NRS]

GORDON, MARY, in Banff, daughter of Charles Gordon of Buthlaw, testament, 1795, Comm. Aberdeen. [NRS]

GORDON, MAXWELL, a Writer to the Signet, son of William Gordon of Nethermuir, Aberdeenshire, was admitted as a Notary Public on 7 March 1794, died 24 December 1809. [NRS.NP2.35.143]

GORDON, NORMAN, agent for the North of Scotland Banking Company in Turriff, Aberdeenshire, in 1849. [POD]

GORDON, PATRICK, an Excise officer in Portsoy, Banffshire, testament, 1794, Comm. Aberdeen. [NRS]

GORDON, PATRICK, born 1859, son of John Gordon of Cairnfield, died in Whangerie, New Zealand, in 1885. [S.13066]

GORDON, PETER, of Mosstown, testament, 1795, Comm. Aberdeen. [NRS]

GORDON, THOMAS, in Achtochrach of Glenrinnes, Banffshire, testament, 1795, Comm. Aberdeen. [NRS]

GORDON, THOMAS, son of Reverend George William Algernon Gordon in Keith, Banffshire, died in Port Maria Bay, Jamaica, on 15 June 1807. [SM.69.718]

GORDON, THOMAS, of Park, was admitted as a burgess of Banff in 1811. [BBR]

GORDON, WILLIAM, son of Alexander Gordon in Knock of Glen Muick, Aberdeenshire, was apprenticed to William Leys a cooper in Aberdeen in 1792. [ACA]

GORDON, WILLIAM, a writer in Edinburgh, son of William Gordon a shoemaker in Forres, Moray, was admitted as a Notary Public on 8 June 1799, died 10 February 1818. [NRS.NP2.36.273]

GORDON, WILLIAM, an inn-waiter in Turriff, Aberdeenshire, was victim of an assault there in 1835. [NRS.AD14.35.70]

GORDON, WILLIAM, born 1828, eldest son of William Gordon a butler at Manar, Ballater, Aberdeenshire, died in Manar, Winton, New Zealand, on 20 December 1875. [AJ.6688]

GOWANS, JAMES, a shipmaster in Gourdon, Bervie, Kincardineshire, testament, 1800, Comm. St Andrews. [NRS]

GRANT, ALEXANDER, born 1776 in Banff, a merchant who was naturalised in Charleston, South Carolina, on 2 November 1807. [NARA.M1183.1]

GRANT, ALEXANDER, from Banff, graduated MA from King's College, Aberdeen, on 30 March 1797. [KCA]

GRANT, ALEXANDER, from Banff, graduated MA from King's College, Aberdeen, on 29 March 1798. [KCA]

GRANT, ALEXANDER, born 1820, son of Robert Grant and his wife Eliza Grant, died in Melbourne, Australia, in February 1874. [Inverallen gravestone, Moray]

GRANT, ALEXANDER, from Elgin, Moray, died in South Carolina on 19 August 1827. [Charleston Observor.1.9.1827]

GRANT, ALEXANDER, born 13 June 1813, in Tullochgarm, Strathspey, Moray, resident of Charleston, South Carolina, for ten years, died there on 14 June 1846. [Second Presbyterian gravestone, Charleston, S.C.]

GRANT, ALEXANDER, son of Alexander Grant the Free Church minister in Tarves, from Lumphanan, Aberdeenshire, was educated at Marischal College around 1850, graduated MA from King's College, Aberdeen, in March 1852, later a Free Church missionary in Amoy, China. [KCA][MCA]

GRANT, CHARLES, from Knockando, Banffshire, graduated MA from King's College, Aberdeen, in March 1834, later a schoolmaster in Aberlour, Banffshire. [KCA]

GRANT, DAVID, from Moray, graduated MA from King's College, Aberdeen, on 30 March 1816, later a missionary in India. [KCA]

GRANT, DAVINA, youngest daughter of Robert Grant of Kincorth, married Frederick Grant from Quebec, at Kincorth, Aberdeenshire, on 9 November 1819. [EA.5840.319]

GRANT, DONALD, from Cromdale, Moray, a mason in Halifax, Nova Scotia, probate, 1848, Halifax, N.S.

GRANT, FRANCIS W., born 1787, formerly minister of Dallas, Moray, minister of Banff from 1821 until 1843 when he joined the Free Church, husband of Sophia Rannie daughter of Thomas Rannie in Cullen, he died on 12 April 1858. [AOB.ii.115]

GRANT, Reverend George, in Rathven, Aberdeenshire, testament, 1790, Comm. Aberdeen. [NRS]

GRANT, Mrs ISABEL, born 1796 in Keith, Banffshire, wife of Peter Grant, died in Halifax, Nova Scotia, on 29 November 1843. [HJ.4.12.1843]

GRANT, JAMES, son of Charles Grant in Cromdale, Strathspey, Moray, was apprenticed to William Cleriheugh, a barber in Edinburgh, for six years, on 2 June 1796. [ERA]

GRANT, JAMES, from Banff, graduated MA from King's College, Aberdeen, in March 1796. [KCA]

GRANT, JAMES, born 1783, son of James Grant, [1747-1792], a farmer, and his wife Jean Fraser, [1743-190], a wright in North Carolina, died in 1828. [Cromdale gravestone, Moray]

GRANT, JAMES, from Moray, graduated MA from King's College, Aberdeen, on 28 March 1799. [KCA]

GRANT, JAMES, from Moray, graduated MA from King's College, Aberdeen, in March 1833, later a minister in Kirkmichael. [KCA]

GRANT, JAMES, in Windsor Park, St Catherine's, Jamaica, son of James Grant tacksman of Midfodderlatter, Banffshire, a deed in 1813. [NRS.RD3.44.858]

GRANT, JAMES MCDOWAL, son of David Grant of Arndilly, Banffshire, was educated at Marischal College around 1820, graduated MA, an evangelist, a planter in Jamaica. [MCA]

GRANT, JAMES, agent in Elgin, Moray, for the Caledonian Banking Company in 1849. [POD]

GRANT, JOHN, son of James Grant of Delchloy, Moray, a writer in Edinburgh, was admitted as a Notary Public on 8 August 1789, was appointed Commissary of Elfin and Forres in 1791, was found guilty of forgery and uttering was sentenced to be transported to the colonies for life in 1793. [NRS.NP2.34.127; PS3.11A.1791.10]

GRANT, JOHN, a blacksmith at the Mains of Muiresk, Turriff, Aberdeenshire, was accused of assault in 1818. [NRS.AD14.18.219]

GRANT, JOHN, a merchant from Elgin, Moray, settled in New York, died on a voyage from N.Y. to Charleston, South Carolina, on 7 March 1839. [AJ.4766]

GRANT, JOHN, agent in Grantown, Strathspey, for the National Bank of Scotland in 1849. [POD]

GRANT, LEWIS, son of Reverend Patrick Grant in Nigg, died on Holiday Hill Estate, Jamaica, on 21 April 1822. [BM.12.129]

GRANT, MARGARET, wife of James Watt a tanner on the burgh muir of Inverurie, Inverurie, Aberdeenshire, was accused of wilful fire-raising in 1828, case not proven. [NRS.JC26.1828.77]

GRANT, PETER, and Isabella Scott, both from Keith, Banffshire, were married in Halifax, Nova Scotia, on 8 January 1829. [AR.17.1.1829]

GRANT, THOMAS, son of Archibald Grant in Keith, Banffshire, died on Bance Island, West Africa, testament, 1793, Comm. Edinburgh. [NRS]

GRANT, WILLIAM, born 15 June 1744 in Blairfindie, Banffshire, son of William Grant and his wife Jean Tyrie, emigrated to Quebec in 1759, a merchant who died there on 5 October 1805. [DCB]

GRANT, WILLIAM, born 1749 in Strathspey, Moray, a former soldier of the 71st Highland Regiment, settled in Charlotte County, New Brunswick, died in Old Ridge, St Stephen, New Brunswick, on 23 May 1831. [NBC.4.6.1831]

GRANT, WILLIAM, son of Donald Grant in Inveravon, Moray, a student in Marischal College in 1790s. [MCA]

GRANT, WILLIAM, a journeyman blacksmith, at the Mains of Muiresk, Turriff, Aberdeenshire, was accused of assault in 1818. [NRS.AD14.18.219]

GRAY, ANN, born 1742, died 1 March 1821, wife of James Mutch in Ironside of New Deer, Aberdeenshire. [New Deer gravestone]

GRAY, Reverend ARCHIBALD, DD, born 1764 in Forres, Moray, died in Halifax, Nova Scotia, on 16 September 1826. [AR.16.9.1826]

GRAY, FRANCIS, born 1842, son of Alexander Gray, [1801-1876], a baker in Aboyne, and his wife Margaret Harley, [1808-1882], died in Australia on 12 August 1873. [Aboyne gravestone, Aberdeen]

GRAY, GEORGE, born 1846, son of Alexander Gray, [1801-1876], a baker in Aboyne, and his wife Margaret Harley, [1808-1882], drowned at Quebec on 25 May 1889. [Aboyne gravestone, Aberdeen]

GRAY, JAMES, born 1778, crofter in Hallgreen, died 20 November 1828, husband of Margaret McPherson, born 1774, died 5 November 1864. [Ruthven gravestone, Aberdeenshire]

GRAY, JAMES, master of the Lady Charlotte of Peterhead in 1784, a sasine, 1794. [AJ.1884][NRS.RS.Aberdeen.1295]

GRAY, JOHN, in Gateside of Pitullie, testament, 1799, Comm. Aberdeen. [NRS]

GRAY, JOHN, born 1837, son of Alexander Gray, [1801-1876], a baker in Aboyne, and his wife Margaret Harley, [1808-1882], died in Sydney, New South Wales, Australia on 28 December 1879. [Aboyne gravestone, Aberdeenshire]

GRAY, ROBERT, a merchant in Ellon, Aberdeenshire, testament, 1794, Comm. Aberdeen. [NRS]

GREEN, JAMES, [1813-1900], a carpenter in Fochabers, Moray, and his wife Susan Bremner, [1804-1858], were parents of George Green, born 1835, who died in Bernardstown, Massachusetts, on 1 July 1860. [Bellie gravestone, Moray]

GREEN, R., agent in Keith, Banffshire, for the Aberdeen Banff in 1849. [POD]

GREIG, JAMES, in Ardluthie, Fetteresso, Kincardineshire, was accused of assault and battery in 1821. [NRS.AD14,21.130]

GRIGOR, JOHN, in Nairnshire, graduated MD from King's College, Aberdeen, on 26 July 1847. [KCA]

GRIGOR, ROBERT, a writer in Edinburgh, son of Robert Grigor a shoemaker in Elgin, Moray, was admitted as a Notary Public on 5 July 1793, died 31 October 1854. [NRS.NP2.35.83]

GRIGOR, ROBERT, son of Robert Grigor a writer in Elgin, Moray, a student at Marischal College around 1830, later a sugar refiner in Jamaica. [MCA]

GRUER, ALEXANDER DUFF, born 1839, fifth son of W. Gruer a farmer in Castleton, Braemar, Aberdeenshire, died at 100 Liverpool Street, Sydney, New South Wales, Australia, on 27 April 1867. [AJ.6235]

HACKET, ..., master of the Betty of Fraserburgh trading between Aberdeen and Bergen, Norway, in 1790. [AJ.2225]

HACKET, PETER, and Elisabeth Rennie, both in Rosehearty, Aberdeenshire, were married in Fraserburgh, Aberdeenshire. on 9 September 1790. [Fraserburgh Episcopal Records]

HADDEN, ROBERT, a weaver in Peterhead, Aberdeenshire, father of George Hadden a shipmaster in London, a sasine, 1798. [NRS.RS.Aberdeen.1825]

HAMILTON, WILLIAM, harpooner of the Robert of Peterhead, Aberdeenshire, was whaling off Greenland or the Davis Strait in 1791. [NRS.E508.91.8]

HARDIE, ALEXANDER, son of Alexander Hall in New Deer, Aberdeenshire, graduated MA from Marischal College in 1818, later a teacher. [MCA]

HARDIE, ALEXANDER MCGRUER, born 1848, son of William Hardie in Knaps, Ellon, Aberdeenshire, died in Brooklyn, New York, on 23 April 1872. [AJ.15.5.1872]

HARDIE, JAMES, a merchant later a shoemaker in Old Meldrum, Aberdeenshire, testament, 1800, Comm. Aberdeen. [NRS]

HARDIE, JAMES, a planter in Jamaica, grandson and heir of James Hardie a carrier in Elgin, Moray, 1848. [NRS.S/H]

HARLAW, JOHN, in Montserrat, British West Indies, son and heir of Alexander Harlaw a merchant in Fraserburgh, Aberdeenshire, in 1789. [NRS.S/H]

HARROW, WILLIAM, a shoemaker, and Agnes Murdoch, both in Fraserburgh, Aberdeenshire, were married there on 10 January 1793. [Fraserburgh Episcopal Records]

HARVEY, JOHN, a Central Railway man in Michigan, son and heir of Charles Harvey a feuar in Huntly, Aberdeenshire, who died on 13 December 1861. [NRS.S/H]

HAY, ADAM, youngest son of John Hay of Braco, Banffshire, died in Lansquinet, Trelawney, Jamaica, on 27 October 1807. [SM.68.398]

HAY, ALEXANDER GEORGE, in Montserrat, British West Indies, grandson and heir to his grandmother Elizabeth Hay, wife of Alexander Hay of Lickliehead, Aberdeenshire, 1801. [NRS.S/H]

HAY, ALEXANDER, born 1807 in Auldearn, Nairn, emigrated to America in June 1828, was naturalised in Union, South Carolina, on 25 July 1838. [Union County Naturalisation petition 19]

HAY, ANDREW, of Rannas, testament, 1791, Comm. Aberdeen. [NRS]

HAY, CHARLES H., a teacher of English in Banff in 1844. [AOB.ii.207]

HAY, GEORGE, in Denhead of Gask, testament, 1793, Comm. Aberdeen. [NRS]

HAY, JAMES, a fisherman in Banff, then in the Seatown of Cullen, was ordered to be apprehended for not fulfilling a contract, in 1812. [Annals of Banff.i.351]

HAY, JAMES, second son of James Hay in Greenacres, Banffshire, died in Toowomba Hospital, Queensland, Australia, on 18 November 1866. [AJ.6220]

HAY, JOHN, son of Patrick Hay a merchant in Deer, Aberdeenshire, graduated MA from Marischal College in 1833, later a missionary in Vizagapatam, Madras, India, who translated the Bible into Teloogg, in 1832 he graduated DD from Rutgers College in New Jersey. [MCA]

HAY, JOHN, from Tarves, Aberdeenshire, graduated MA from King's College, Aberdeen, in March 1834, later in Sydney, New South Wales, Australia. [KCA]

HAY, Major PATRICK, in the Service of the East India Company, a sasine, Elgin, Moray, 1794. [NRS.R.S.Elgin.368]

HAY, RACHEL, daughter of James Hay in Banff, wife of Jonathan Ludford, ded in Spanish Town, Jamaica, on 18 December 1802. [EEC.14226]

HAY, Captain, WILLIAM, from Garmouth, Moray, married Elizabeth Dodd from Islington, London, in Sydney, New South Wales, Australia, on 4 January 1840. [AJ.4830]

HEATON, JOHN, a farmer in Oldwhat, testament, 1794, Comm. Aberdeen. [NRS]

HENDERSON, ALEXANDER, a merchant in St Kitts, was admitted as a burgess of Banff in 1770. [BBR]

HENDERSON, JAMES, son of William Henderson in Auchlunies, was apprenticed to William Bain a weaver in Aberdeen, in 1791. [ACA]

HENDERSON, WILLIAM, a merchant in Fraserburgh, Aberdeen, testament, 1800, Comm. Aberdeen. [NRS] Aberdeenshire, testament, 1792, Comm. Aberdeen. [NRS]

HENDRY, ANDREW, a shipmaster in Peterhead, Aberdeenshire, husband of Margaret Duguid testament, 1796, Comm. Aberdeen. [NRS]

HENDRY, GEORGE, in Old Maud, Aberdeenshire, testament, 1795, Comm. Aberdeen. [NRS]

HENDRY, JEAN, in Mormond, Strichen, Aberdeenshire, testament, 1795, Comm. Aberdeen. [NRS]

HENDRY, ROBERT, a victim of crime in 1837. [NRS.JC26.1837.62]

HENRY, LEWIS, born 1778 in Aberdeenshire, a merchant in Newcastle, New Brunswick, died there on 17 March 1836, [GNS.22.3.1836]

HOGARTH, WILLIAM, son of William Hogarth a merchant in Aberdeen, was educated at Marischal College in 1850s, later a sheep farmer in Queensland, Australia. [MCA]

HORN, WILLIAM, son of James Horn in Bonnytown, Mill, Rayne, Aberdeenshire, was apprenticed to William Logan a merchant in Aberdeen in 1792. [ACA]

HOWAT, JOHN, in Wabashaw, America, cousin and heir of John Howat a farmer in Kincuichland, Banffshire, 1860. [NRS.S/H]

HOUSTON, CLEMENTINA, eldest daughter of Alexander Houston in Grantown, married Patrick Cruikshank of St Vincent, in 1813, [EA.5182.13]

HUME, CHARLES, in Netherton of Lethenty, Daviot, Aberdeenshire, testament, 1797, Comm. Aberdeen. [NRS]

HUNTER, JOHN, in Blairdens Mill, testament, 1795, Comm. Aberdeen. [NRS]

HUNTER, JOHN, a merchant in Meikle Gourdas, Aberdeenshire, testament, 1799, Comm. Aberdeen. [NRS]

HUNTER, WILLIAM, in Broomhillock, testament, 1800, Comm. Aberdeen. [NRS]

HUNTER, WILLIAM CHALMERS, son of John Hunter of Tillery, Udny, Aberdeenshire, graduated MA from Marischal College in 1818. [MCA]

HUTCHEON, JAMES, a merchant in Tarland, Aberdeenshire, testament, 1795, Comm. Aberdeen. [NRS]

HUTCHESON, ALEXANDER, son of Reverend John Hutcheson in Fetteresso, Kincardineshire, died in Kingstown, St Vincent, in 1812. [EA.5118.13]

HUTCHISON, ALFRED, son of James Hutchison a merchant in Peterhead, Aberdeenshire, a student at Marischal College in 1850s, later a tea merchant in Hong Kong and Canton, China. [MCA]

HUTCHISON, JOHN, a shipmaster in Peterhead, Aberdeenshire, son of Robert Hutchison a shipmaster in Peterhead, in 1792. [NRS.RS.Aberdeen.1097]

HUTCHISON, ROBERT, a skipper in Peterhead, inventory, 1801, Comm. Aberdeen. [NRS]

HUTCHESON, PETER, a merchant in Peterhead, Aberdeenshire, testament, 1795, Comm. Aberdeen. [NRS]

HUTCHISON, WILLIAM, a skipper in Peterhead, Aberdeenshire, son of James Hutchison a merchant there, inventory, 1819, Comm. Aberdeen. [NRS]

HUTTON, JAMES, born 1819, son of James Hutton in Aberdeenshire, died in Halifax, Nova Scotia, on 2 April 1836. [NSRG.6.4.1836]

IMLACH, JAMES, of Banff, married Isabella Elizabeth Leslie, daughter of Reverend William Leslie of Balnageith, Moray, in St Martin's Church, London, on 10 June 1820. [SM.86.94]

INGRAM, GEORGE, from Banff, a smith in Trinidad, nephew and heir of George Ingram a feuar in Macduff, Banffshire, 1842. [NRS.S/H]

INNES, ALEXANDER, born in Bridgend of Glenlivet, Banffshire, settled in America in 1840, an innkeeper who died in Port Dover, Canada West, on 17 April 1860. [GM.NS2/9.210]

INNES, ELIZABETH, widow of Revered William Cumming at Mill of Turriff, Aberdeenshire, testament, 1791, Comm. Aberdeen. [NRS]

INNES, GEORGE, born 1781 in Banffshire, died in Wilmot, Nova Scotia, on 28 July 1834. [NBC.23.8.1834]

INNES, GEORGE, son of George Innes in Huntly, Aberdeenshire, a student in Marischal College, graduated MA in 1794. [MCA]

INNES, JOHN, son of Sir Gordon Innes of Coxtown, died in Kingston, Jamaica, in 1800. [SM.62.576]

INNES, JOSEPH, of Pitmedden, Aberdeenshire, testament, 1800, Comm. Aberdeen. [NRS]

INNES, MARY, daughter of Alexander Innes of Pitmeddan, Aberdeenshire, died in Aberdeen on 3 June 1820. [SM.86.190]

INNES, ROBERT, son of Robert Innes a farmer in Rathen, Aberdeenshire, graduated MA from Marischal College in 1818, later a schoolmaster in Cullen, Banffshire. [MCA]

INNES, R., agent in Inverury, Aberdeenshire, for the Aberdeen Bank in 1849. [POD]

INNES, WILLIAM, from Demerara, married Eliza Donaldson, daughter of William Donaldson, in Elgin, Moray, in July 1801. [GC.1547]

IRVINE, ALEXANDER, of Drum, Aberdeenshire, was appointed a trustee of Dr John Anderson in St Kitts, British West Indies, in 1791. [NRS.RD3.253.542]

IRVINE, ARCHIBALD KENNEDY, in Kincardineshire, graduated MD from King's College, Aberdeen, on 3 August 1849. [KCA]

IRVINE, FRANCIS baptised on 8 February 1786, son of Alexander Irvine of Drum, Aberdeenshire, and his wife Jean Forbes, a soldier from 1804 until 1820, a Captain of the Bengal Army, died 16 December 1855 in Edinburgh. [BA.2.529]

IRVINE, GEORGE, of Boyndlie, Aberdeenshire, testament, 1798, Comm. Aberdeen. [NRS]

JACK, JOHN, and Isaac Forsyth, were granted a lease of land in Lossiemouth, Moray, as a coal store, on 5 March 1798. [Records of Elgin.i.507]

JACKSON, ALEXANDER, from Keith, Banffshire, a carpenter with the Ordnance Department in Halifax, Nova Scotia, probate, 1818, Halifax, N.S.

JAFFRAY, ALEXANDER, in Old Meldrum, Aberdeenshire, testament, 1798, Comm. Aberdeen. [NRS]

JAFFRAY, MARY, in Corthies, testament, 1791, Comm. Aberdeen. [NRS]

JAMES, ANDREW, master of the <u>Anne of Portsoy,</u> Banffshire, trading between Fort William an Inverness in 1812. [NRS.E504.17.8]

JAMES, JOHN, son of Thomas James in Kincardine, was apprenticed to William Strachan a baker in Aberdeen in 1791. [ACA]

JAMES, JOHN, a skipper in Garmouth, testament, 1802, Comm. Moray. [NRS]

JAMIESON, ALEXANDER, son of John Jamieson a merchant in Elgin, Moray, died in Clarendon, Jamaica, in January 1804. [SM.66.238]

JAMESON, JAMES, born 1843, son of James Jameson [1806-1895] and his wife Isabel Carnie [1822-1889], died in Barre, Vermont, on 7 May 1900. [Banchory Ternan gravestone, Kincardineshire]

JAMIESON, JOHN, in Upper Kebbary, Midmar, Aberdeenshire, testament, 1799, Comm. Aberdeen. [NRS]

JAMIESON, JOHN COUTTS, in Goshen, Jamaica, son and heir of Andrew Jamieson a merchant in Turriff, Aberdeenshire, 1850. [NRS.S/H]

JAMIESON, MARY, from Banffshire, married Godfrey M. Schwartz in Halifax, New Brunswick on 23 December 1843. [HT.26.12.1843]

JAMIESON, ROBERT, from Moray, graduated MA from King's College, Aberdeen, on 29 March 1793. [KCA]

JAMIESON, THOMAS ABERCROMBIE, son of George Jamieson a merchant in Fordyce, Banffshire, a writer in Banff who was admitted as a Notary Public on 15 May 1790. [NRS.SC2.19.1; NP2.34.169]

JAMIESON, WILLIAM, from Banff, graduated MA from King's College, Aberdeen, in March 1826, later was the British chaplain in Amsterdam, Holland. [KCA]

JOHNSTON, GEORGE, son of George Johnston in Portsoy, Banffshire, was apprenticed to John Hall, a merchant in Edinburgh, for five years, on 31 October 1799. [ERA]

JOHNSTON, HUGH, born 1755 in Moray, died in St John, New Brunswick, on 29 November 1829. [NBC.5.12.1829]

JOHNSTON, JAMES, minister at Crimond, Aberdeenshire, testament, 1796, Comm. Aberdeen. [NRS]

JOHNSTON, JAMES, a farmer in the Oldtown of Ardendraught, testament, 1800, Comm. Aberdeen. [NRS]

JOHNSTON, JOHN, son of James Johnston in Bogfairley, was apprenticed to William Seaton a baker in Aberdeen in 1793. [ACA]

JOHNSTON, JOHN, son of George Johnston a farmer in Evertoun of Auchnagatt, graduated MA from Marischal College in 1854, later a banker in Milwaukee, Wisconsin. [MCA]

JOHNSTON, Mrs KATHERINE, at Lochead, relict of James Johnston a bleacher there, testament, 1800, Comm. Aberdeen. [NRS]

JOHNSTON, WILLIAM, an elder of the parish of Banff in 1834. [AOB.ii.116]

JOHNSTON, ..., master of the Lovely Charlotte of Portsoy, Banffshire, was shipwrecked at Montrose, Angus, in 1790. [AJ.2236]

JUNOR, HUGH, in New Mill, Strichen, Aberdeenshire, father of Mary Wyllie Junor who married Thomas Woodman of Plantation Adelphi, Berbice, in Georgetown, Demerara, on 3 September 1878, she died there on 4 February 1880. [S.10984/11430]

JOPP, ANDREW, an advocate in Aberdeen, son of Alexander Jopp at Insch, Aberdeenshire, was admitted as a Notary Public on 6 July 1796, died 9 June 1829. [NRS.NP2.36.7]

KEITH, DAVID, son of Dr Alexander Keith a minister in St Cyrus, Kincardineshire, graduated MA from Marischal College in 1847 and MD from Edinburgh University in 1851, later was a surgeon in the Service of the East India Company, [MCA]

KEITH, JAMES, formerly in Charleston, South Carolina, latterly in Blairshinnock, Banffshire, admin. 1810, PCC. [TNA]

KEITH, LEWIS, born 1806 in Elgin, Moray, died in Halifax, Nova Scotia, on 1 June 1843. [Halifax Times, 6.6.1843]

KEITH, WILLIAM SIM, born 1789, of the Malta Civil Service, died 17 January 1857. [Ruthven gravestone, Aberdeenshire]

KELMAN, JOHN, son of William Kelman a merchant in Fraserburgh, Aberdeenshire, was educated at Marischal College around 1816, later an assistant surgeon in the Service of the East India Company. [MCA]

KELMAN, WILLIAM, a writer in Aberdeen, son of William Kelman a farmer in Ellon, Aberdeenshire, was admitted as a Notary Public on 27 January 1796. [NRS.NP2.35.295]

KETCHEN, JAMES, from Nairn, graduated MA from King's College, Aberdeen, on 30 March 1804, later in the Service of the Honourable East India Company. [KCA]

KIDD, JAMES, from New Deer, Aberdeenshire, graduated MA from King's College, Aberdeen, in March 1851, later a minister in New Brunswick. [KCA]

KING, CHARLES, a merchant in Peterhead, Aberdeenshire, a decreet, 1841. [NRS.CS38.14.42]

KINLOCH, LOCKHART, a writer in Inverness, son of William Kinloch a tailor in Nairn, was admitted as a Notary Public on 9 July 1795, died on 16 May 1831. [NRS.NP2.35.261]

KIRTON, GEORGE, born 1835, a butcher from Ellon, Aberdeenshire, died in Toonookoo, New South Wales, Australia, on 9 December 1866. [AJ.6217]

KIRTON, JOHN, son and heir to his mother Barbara Anderson or Kirton or Castor of Tushielaw, widow of Alexander Kirton in Barbados, who died in 1790. [NRS.S/H.1793]

KITCHEN, ISAAC, born 1750, for 40 years minister of the Secession Church in Nairn, died there on 12 May 1820. [SM.86.96]

KNIGHT, ADAM, from Portsoy, Banffshire, died in Demerara in 1808. [SM.70.477]

KNIGHT, ROBERT, a minister in Canada, nephew and heir of Elizabeth Knight in Portsoy, Banffshire, 1842. [NRS.S/H]

KYNOCH, JOHN, was appointed church beadle of Banff in 1836. [AOB.ii.119]

LABBAN, ……, master of the Friendship of Buckie, from Aberdeen bound for Inverness in 1790. [AJ.2228]

LAING, JOHN, a skipper in Macduff, inventory, 1822, Comm. Aberdeen. [NRS]

LAING, MARIA, born 1778, widow of John Laing of Haddo, Aberdeenshire, and Dominica, died in Jersey on 22 February 1853. [GM.NS39.452]

LAING, WILLIAM, born in Fraserburgh, Aberdeenshire, was educated at King's College, Aberdeen, and graduated MA from Marischal College, Aberdeen, in 1782, a schoolmaster at Aberdeen Grammar School, later Episcopal minister in Peterhead from 1771 until his death in 1812. [NRS.CH12.15.48]; a letter dated 1803. [NRS.CH12.12.2135]

LAIRD, CLAUD, son of John Laird a merchant in Forres, Moray, a writer in Forres, was admitted as a Notary Public on 18 May 1791. [NRS.NP2.34.243]

LAMB, JOHN, born in Findhorn, Moray, a mariner who was naturalised in Charleston, South Carolina, on 19 March 1804. [NARA.M1183.1]

LAMB, ROBERT, a clerk in New York, son and heir of Robert Lamb a merchant in Elgin, Moray, who died on 6 February 1857. [NRS.S/H]

LAMONT, CHARLES, from Aberdeenshire, married Mary Frances Grant from Halifax, Nova Scotia, there on 17 January 1838. [HP.27.1.1838]

LARGIE, JOHN, a shipmaster in Gourdon, Bervie, Kincardineshire, a testament, 1793, Comm. St Andrews. [NRS]

LAUGHTON, JOHN, a skipper in Findhorn, testament, 1825, Comm. Moray. [NRS]

LAURENCE, ALEXANDER, born 1798 in Peterhead, Aberdeenshire, son of Charles Laurence and his wife Margaret Yule, a stonecutter in New York, died at 17 Wooster Street, N.Y. on 3 March 1853. [ANY]

LAURENCE, ANDREW, born 3 April 1785 in Dunnottar, son of Catharine Beattie, died in Trinidad on 10 August 1802. [Dunnottar gravestone, Kincardineshire]

LAURENCE, JOHN, son of William Laurence a turner in Banff, a writer in Banff, was admitted as a Notary Public on 10 July 1790. [NRS.NP2.34.201]

LAW, GEORGE, born 1768, a shipmaster in Stonehaven, died in 1832. [Fetteresso gravestone, Kincardineshire]

LAW, WILLIAM, a skipper in Stonehaven, testament, 1808, Comm. St Andrews. [NRS]

LAWSON, JOHN, jr., son of John Lawson a farmer in Elgin, Moray, was educated at Marischal College from 1812 to 1815, a banker and Provost of Elgin, Moray, married Margaret Helen Walker, eldest daughter of Reverend Alexander Walker of Elgin, there on 12 January 1826; agent in Elgin for the Commercial Bank of Scotland in 1849. [SM.97.254][MCA][POD]

LAWSON, WILLIAM, a writer in Edinburgh, son of John Lawson a farmer in Auchrisk, Banffshire, was admitted as a Notary Public on 2 July 1796, died 29 April 1807. [NRS.NP2.35.349]

LAWSON, WILLIAM, Episcopalian minister of Old Deer, Aberdeenshire, from 1816 until 1827.

LAWTIE, GEORGE, born 1725, Customs officer in Banff, died 11 March 1799, husband of Grizel Urquhart. [Banff gravestone]

LAWTIE, PETER, born 25 February 1792 in Banff, son of G.U. Lawtie and his wife Sarah, a Lieutenant of the Corps of Engineers in the Bengal Army, died on 5 May 1815 in the Nepal War. [Banff parish church]

LEASK, JOHN, a teacher in Banff in 1847. [AOB.ii.207]

LEASK, WILLIAM, in New York, heir to his grand-uncle John Leask a merchant in Macduff, Banffshire, who died on 4 May 1844. [NRS.S/H]

LEDINGHAM, WILLIAM, and his wife Margaret Bartlett, parents of William Ledingham, a merchant in Buenos Ayres, Argentina, who died there in 1871. [Dyce gravestone, Aberdeenshire]

LEES, ALEXANDER, born 1723, a seaman in Cowie, died 11 March 1804. [Cowie gravestone, Kincardineshire]

LEIPER, ALEXANDER, born 1732, a whitefisher in Findon, died 1 June 1804. [Banchory Devenick gravestone, Kincardineshire]

LEIPER, GEORGE, born 1716, a whitefisher in Findon, died 1812. [Banchory Devenick gravestone, Kincardineshire]

LEIPER, JAMES, born 1750, a whitefisher in Burnbank, died 23 February 1840. [Port Lethan gravestone, Kincardineshire]

LEITH, ALEXANDER, born 1811, son of Alexander Leith, [1757-1845], and his wife Elizabeth Booth, [1772-1862], died in Melbourne, Victoria, Australia, on 13 February 1868. [Marnoch gravestone, Banffshire]

LEITH, A.H., in Aberdeenshire, graduated MD from King's College, Aberdeen, on 6 April 1847. [KCA]

LEITH, FRANCIS, a writer in Aberdeen, son of John Leith a messenger in Old Meldrum, Aberdeenshire, was admitted as a Notary Public on 2 March 1792. [NRS.NP2.34.325]

LEITH, GEORGE, in Banffshire, graduated MD from King's College, Aberdeen, on 30 July 1845. [KCA]

LEITH, GEORGE, born 1815, son of Alexander Leith, [1757-1845], and his wife Elizabeth Booth, [1772-1862], died in Largie, Canada, on 28 December 1881. [Marnoch gravestone, Banffshire]

LEITH, JOHN, a surgeon in Spanish Town, Jamaica, son of James Leith of Whiterigside, Aberdeenshire, a deed, 1790. [NRS.RD4.249.1183]

LEITH, S., teacher of drawing in Banff in 1830. [AOB.ii.207]

LENDRUM, R., agent in Ellon, Aberdeenshire, of the Aberdeen Bank in 1849. [POD]

LESLIE, JAMES, son of James Leslie in Kair, Kincardineshire, was educated at King's College, Aberdeen, from 1801 to 1802, later a merchant in Canada. [KCA]

LESLIE, JAMES WALKER, born 1849, son of John Leslie a surgeon in Inverurie, Aberdeenshire, died on Plantation Belair, Demerara, on 30 September 1872. [AJ.6.11.1872]

LESLIE, JOHN, in Cottburn, Turriff, Aberdeenshire, testament, 1792, Comm. Aberdeen. [NRS]

LESLIE, JOHN, born 1788, died 9 April 1836, husband of Jane Watt, born 1789, died in July 1843. [Banff gravestone]

LESLIE, JOHN, a merchant in Peterhead, Aberdeenshire, a decreet, 1816. [NRS.CS42.21.86]

LESLIE, PATRICK, son of William Leslie of Warthill a gentleman, a student at Marischal College in 1830s, later settled in New South Wales, Australia. [MCA]

LESLIE, ROBERT, a merchant in Monymusk, Aberdeenshire, testament, 1799, Comm. Aberdeen. [NRS]

LESLIE, WILLIAM, an elder of the parish of Banff in 1834. [AOB.ii.116]

LESLIE, Captain, master of the <u>Empress of Banff</u> from Stromness with passengers bound for Quebec in 1852, also in 1853 and 1854. [QM]

LEYS, JOHN, baptised 17 June 1785 in Crathie, Aberdeenshire, son of Francis Leys in Inver and his wife Janet Michie, a soldier from 1800 until his death at Fatehgarh on 14 December 1826, a Lieutenant Colonel of the 29th Native Infantry of the Bengal Army. [BA.3.50]

LIGERTWOOD, ALEXANDER, son of William Ligertwood of Logiereve, Udny, Aberdeenshire, a student at Marischal College around 1850, later in New Zealand. [MCA]

LIDGERWOOD, JOHN, born 1795 in Longside, Aberdeenshire, a mason later a merchant who emigrated via Liverpool to America, was naturalised in 1829 in New York. [NY Court of Common Pleas]

LILLIE, ALEXANDER, a merchant, was ordained as an elder in Banff on 21 March 1841. [AOB.ii.122]

LILLIE, ALEXANDER, son of Alexander Lillie a merchant in Banff, a student a Marischal College in 1830s, later a merchant in Melbourne, Victoria, Australia. [MCA]

LILLIE, or STROTHER, MARGARET, in Petty, Inverness-shire, sister and heir of Jessie Lillie from Forres, Moray, later in Kingston, Jamaica, who died on 6 January 1832. [NRS.S/H]

LILLIE, WILLIAM, in the Kirkton of St Fergus, Aberdeenshire, testament, 1792, Comm. Aberdeen. [NRS]

LILLIE, WILLIAM, son of Alexander Lillie a merchant in Banff, graduated MA from Marischal College in 1839, later a banker in South Africa and in London. [MCA]

LITTLEJOHN, THOMAS, a storekeeper in St John, New Brunswick, son and heir of John Littlejohn a shoemaker in Torry, Aberdeenshire, who died on 20 November 1856. [NRS.S/H]

LIVINGSTONE, CHRISTIAN, relict of Captain William Whyte a shipmaster in Peterhead, testament, 1807, Comm. Aberdeen. [NRS]

LOBBAN, GEORGE, born 1799, died in November 1878, husband of Isabella Joss, born 1812, died in January 1871. [Mortlach gravestone, Banffshire]

LOBBAN, JOSEPH, born 1846, a shoemaker in Aberchirder, died 6 July 1916, husband of Isabella Williamson, born 1850, died 14 June 1887. [Mortlach gravestone, Banffshire]

LOGIE, JAMES, from Moray, graduated MA from King's College, Aberdeen, on 29 March 1802, later schoolmaster at Knockando. [KCA]

LONGMORE, GEORGE, from Banff, graduated MA from King's College, Aberdeen, In March 1796. [KCA]

LONGMORE, JOHN, in Milton of Deskford, Banffshire, testament, 1800, Comm. Aberdeen. [NRS]

LONGMORE, WILLIAM, agent in Keith, Banffshire, for the North of Scotland Banking Company, in 1849. [POD]

LONGMUIR, ALEXANDER, master of the <u>Gazelle of Peterhead</u> from Peterhead with passengers bound for Port Philip and Melbourne, Australia, in April 1853, landed in Melbourne, Victoria, on 20 October 1853. [AJ.5489/5535]

LONGMUIR, ANDREW, born 1761, son of John Longmuir and his wife Elizabeth Collie, a shipmaster in Aberdeen who died in Leith in 1802. [Fetteresso gravestone, Kincardineshire]

LOVIE, WILLIAM, a shipmaster in Whitehills, Banffshire, a sasine 1791. [NRS.RS,Banff.251]

LOW, GEORGE, a slater in Fraserburgh, Aberdeenshire, married Mary Milne, there on 4 August 1799. [NRS.CH12.32.2]

LOW, JAMES, born 1727, an architect in Fraserburgh, Aberdeenshire, died 2 June 1814, husband of Ann Beattie, born 1732, died 1825. [Kirkton, Fraserburgh, gravestone]

LOW JOHN, son of Robert Low in Balfife, Kincardineshire, a writer in Aberdeen, was admitted as a Notary Public on 30 June 1791. [NRS.NP2.34.269]

LOW, JOHN, a farmer in Cairnorie, testament, 1799, Comm. Aberdeen. [NRS]

LOW, MARGARET, in Fraserburgh, Aberdeenshire, was accused of mobbing and rioting there in 1813. [NRS.AD4.13.88]

LOW, ROBERT SPARK, born 1837, son of John Low and his wife Rebecca Alexander, died in Wanganui, New Zealand, on 8 November 1875. [Laurencekirk gravestone]

LUMSDEN, JOHN TOWER, son of Henry Tower of Tillwhilly an advocate in Aberdeen, a student at Marischal College in 1840, later a Lieutenant of the East India Company who was killed at Lucknow, India, in 1857. [MCA]

LUMSDEN, THOMAS, born 12 June 1789, son of Harry Lumsden of Belhelvie and Pitcaple, and his wife Catherine McVeagh, a Colonel of the Bengal Army, died at Belhelvie, Aberdeenshire, on 8 December 1874. [BA.3.96]

LYELL, Major GEORGE, of Kinneff, Kincardineshire, father of George Simpson Lyell born 1826, later in Sydney, New South Wales, Australia, 1861, who died there on 29 October 1884. [NRS.S/H][S.12947]

LYELL, JOHN THOMAS STUART, a surgeon, eldest son of George Lyell of Kinneff, Kincardineshire, died in Demerara on 3 December 1836. [AJ.4640]

LYELL, Mrs, widow of John Lyall in Van Diemen's Land, Australia, died in Balmakewan, Kincardineshire, on 24 January 1856. [AJ.5638]

LYNCH, MARY ANN, daughter of W. H. Lynch in Clarendon, Jamaica, niece and heir of Alexander Skene of Marcus, of the Royal Navy in 1829. [NRS.S/H]

LYON, CHRISTINA, born 1831, daughter of Alexander Lyon and his wife Elizabeth Taylor, died in New Zealand in 1885. [Fetteresso gravestone]

LYON, GEORGE, a baillie and innkeeper in Inverurie, Aberdeenshire, was accused of celebrating a clandestine marriage in 1812. [NRS.AD14.12.30]

LYON, GEORGE, born 1860, son of Alexander Lyon and his wife Elizabeth Taylor, died in Australia on 25 October 1894. [Fetteresso gravestone]

LYON, JAMES, from Banff, graduated MA from King's College, Aberdeen, on 26 March 1790. [KCA]

MCALLISTER, ARCHIBALD, born 1812 in Banffshire, a tinplate worker, was accused of assault in 1832. [NRS.AD14.32.21]

MCANDREW, AENEAS, son of James MacAndrew a gentleman in Elgin, Moray, graduated MA from Marischal College in 1820, and MD from Edinburgh University in 1824, died in Meerut, India. [MCA]

MCANDREW, GEORGE SHIRLEY, son of James McAndrew in Elgin, Moray, formerly in the Royal Navy, died in Goshan, St Ann's, Jamaica, on 27 June 1822. [BM.12.519]

MCANDREW, LUDOVIC, son of James MacAndrew a gentleman in Elgin, Moray, graduated MA from Marischal College in 1821, later a merchant in Lisbon, Portugal. [MCA]

MCANDREW, ROBERT, born 1768, a wright in Aberchirder, Banffshire, died 15 July 1829. [Marnoch gravestone, Banffshire]

MCARTHUR, ALEXANDER, from Nairn, graduated MA from King's College, Aberdeen, on 30 March 1807, later in the Service of the East India Company. [KCA]

MCARTHUR, ALEXANDER, born 1843 in Nairn, emigrated to Canada in 1861, a banker in Toronto from 1861 until 1864, an employee of the Hudson Bay Company from 1864 to 1868, settled in Winnipeg in 1869, manager of the Manitoba Investment Association, died in 1887. [NLS]

MCARTHUR, PETER, from Nairn, graduated MA from King's College, Aberdeen, on 29 March 1793. [KCA]

MCBEAN, JOHN, born 1 April 1811 in Nairn, son of John McBean, graduated MA from King's College, Aberdeen, in March 1832, later a minister in New Brunswick from 1841 to 1847, in Columbo, Ceylon, from 1854 to 1862, in Australia from 1850 to 1884, and from 1862 to 1884, died in North Adelaide, South Australia, on 13 August 1897. [KCA][F.7.593]

MCBEAN, WILLIAM, at Brachlach, Nairn, bound for Roaring Lion River, St Ann's, Jamaica, appointed Jean McBean widow o Valentine White of Brachlach, Lieutenant William White of the 73rd Regiment, and Thomas Alves in Spanish Town, Jamaica, as his attornies in 1789. [NRS.RD3.290.92]

MCBEATH, WILLIAM, from Moray, graduated MA from King's College, Aberdeen, on 30 March 1790. [KCA]

MCEWAN, A., agent of the Commercial Bank of Scotland in Banff in 1849. [POD]

MCCOMBIE, GEORGE, son of George McCombie in Newbigging, was apprenticed to Alexander Dalgarno a merchant in Aberdeen in 1791. [ACA]

MCCOMBIE, THOMAS, born 7 February 1819, son of Charles McCombie and his wife Anne Black, a Member of the Legislature Assembly of Victoria, Australia, died on 2 October 1869. [Tough gravestone]

MCCONACHIE, ALEXANDER, born 7 July 1840 in Glenrinnes, Banffshire, died in Port Angeles, Clallam, Washington, in February 1927.

MCCURRACH, JAMES, an apprentice shoemaker in Elgin, Moray, found guilty of armed assault and sentenced to transportation to the colonies for seven years, at Inverness on 26 April 1811. [SM.83.5/394]

MCDIARMID, ARCHIBALD, from Callander, Perthshire, a teacher of Mathematics in Banff in 1846. [AOB.ii.207]

MCDONALD, DANIEL, from Banff, graduated MA from King's College, Aberdeen, on 29 March 1798. [KCA]

MCDONALD, DONALD, from Inverallan, Banffshire, graduated MA from King's College, Aberdeen, in March 1841, later a surgeon in the Service of the East India Company. [KCA]

MCDONALD, WILLIAM, an engineer in North America, brother and heir of John McDonald a millwright and builder in Newtownhill, Kincardineshire, 1865. [NRS.S/H]

MCDOWELL, WILLIAM, Rector of Banff Grammar School in 1845. [AOB.ii.129]

MCFARLANE, JAMES R., from Crathie, Aberdeenshire, graduated MA from King's College, Aberdeen, in March 1833, later a chaplain in the Service of the East India Company in Madras, India. [KCA]

MCFARLANE, THOMAS, son of Mungo McFarlane a farmer in Boharn, Banffshire, graduated MA from Marischal College in 1851, later a minister in Amsterdam, Holland. [MCA]

MCGILLIVRAY, JOHN, a road surveyor in Nairn, 1846. [NRS.CS280.8.23]

MCGLASHAN, JOHN, son of John McGlashan a brewer in Invernettie, a student at Marischal College in 1850s, later an engineer on the Indian Peninsular Railway. [MCA]

MCGOWAN, BESS, spouse to Robert Garioch a shoemaker in Midmar, Aberdeenshire, testament, 1793, Comm. Aberdeen. [NRS]

MCGREGOR, Captain CHARLES, born 1780, died in Delovar, Banffshire [?], in 1831. [AJ.31.3.1831]

MCGREGOR, DANIEL, from Banff, graduated MA from King's College, Aberdeen, in March 1822, later a schoolmaster in Walton. [KCA]

MCINTOSH, ALEXANDER, from Nairn, graduated MA from King's College, Aberdeen, on 30 March 1797. [KCA]

MACINTOSH, CHARLES, a physician in Jamaica, was admitted as a burgess of Banff in 1770. [BBR]

MACKINTOSH, DANIEL, born 22 March 1756 in Nairnshire, died in Charleston, South Carolina, on 20 February 1839. [Third Presbyterian gravestone, Charleston]

MACINTOSH, HUGH, from Nairn, teacher of English and of Arithmetic in Banff from 1839 to 1843. [AOB.ii.207]

MCINTOSH, JAMES, from Nairn, graduated MA from King's College, Aberdeen, in 1846, later a Free Church missionary in Madras, India. [KCA]

MCINTOSH, JAMES, in Cowhill, Peterhead, Aberdeenshire, victim of assault and robbery in Rose Street, Edinburgh, in 1849. [NRS.JC26.1849.393]

MCINTOSH, JOHN, at the Mill of Corlarach, Aberdeenshire, testament, 1792, Comm. Aberdeen. [NRS]

MCINTOSH, JOHN INNES, from Moray, graduated MA in March 1842, and MD, both from King's College, Aberdeen, on 31 July 1844, settled in England. [KCA]

MCINTOSH, WILLIAM, from Moray, graduated MA from King's College, Aberdeen, on 30 March 1790. [KCA]

MCIRVINE, GEORGE, from Glass, Aberdeenshire, graduated MA from King's College, Aberdeen, later a schoolmaster in Aboyne, Aberdeenshire, then a minister in Mauritius. [KCA]

MACKANDY, ALEXANDER, a shipmaster in Garmouth, Moray, husband of Isobel Wilson, a sasine, 1795. [NRS.RS.Elgin.387]

MACKAY, WILLIAM, a chapman in Fraserburgh, Aberdeenshire, testament, 1790, Comm. Aberdeen. [NRS]

MACKAY, …., master of the John of Banff, trading between Christiansand, Norway, and Newcastle in 1798. [AJ.2646]

MCKENZIE, CHARLES, master of the Witness of Banff from Banff with passengers bound for Melbourne, Victoria, on 17 August 1852, landed there on 24 January 1853. [AJ.5454/5457][LCL.4192]

MACKENZIE, JAMES, born 12 August 1821, son of Roderick Mackenzie of Glack and his wife Christina Niven, a Lieutenant Colonel of the 72nd Highlanders who was killed near Mussuabad. Rajpootana, Bombay, India, on 5 March 1858. [Daviot gravestone]

MCKENZIE, MARY, in Park, Lonmay, Aberdeenshire, testament, 1798, Comm. Aberdeen. [NRS]

MCKENZIE, ROBERT, son of Peter McKenzie, 1808-1871, and his wife Janet Grant, 1811-1853, settled in New South Wales, Australia, before 1886. [Inverallen gravestone, Banffshire]

MACKIE, ALEXANDER, in Corbshill, New Deer, Aberdeenshire, an inventory, 1820, Comm. Aberdeen. [NRS]

MACKIE, ELIZABETH, in Mersea, Ontario, heir to James Mackie in Macduff, Banffshire, who died 24 May 1858. [NRS.S/H]

MACKIE, JAMES, in Ogemaw, Michigan, heir to James Mackie in Macduff, Banffshire, who died 24 May 1858. [NRS.S/H]

MACKIE, Reverend JAMES, born 1820, son of George Mackie in Hillhead of Blackchambers, Kinellar, former minister of Buckie, Banffshire, died at St Mark's Demerara, on 14 April 1876. [F.7.678][AJ.6702]

MCKILLIGAN, WILLIAM ABERCROMBY, born 1803, youngest son of Major McKilligan, died in Banff on 18 December 1825. [SM.97.128]

MCKIMMEY, WILLIAM, born in Rathen, Aberdeenshire, a planter on the May River, South Carolina, died in April 1799. [AJ.2687]

MCKINNON, ALEXANDER, a merchant in Leghorn, [Livorno], Italy, was admitted as a merchant of Banff in 1786. [BBR]

MCKISSACH, JOHN, born 1818, a farmer in the Hillhead of Birnie, Moray, died in Cardigan Terrace, Melbourne, Victoria, Australia, on 21 December 1853. [Birnie gravestone],

MCKISSACK, JOHN, born 1834, son of William McKissack, a millwright in New Elgin, Moray, and his wife Margaret Gow, died in Wairiki, Taviuni, Fiji, on 7 February 1882. [Birnie gravestone, Moray]

MCLAGAN, WILLIAM, from Falkirk, later in Leyhead, Tullich, Aberdeenshire, testament, 1794, Comm. Aberdeen. [NRS]

MACLEAN, GEORGE, son of Reverend James MacLean in Keith, Banffshire, a student at Marischal College around 1817, later Governor of Cape Coast Castle in Africa. [MCA]

MACLEAN, HUGH, son of Reverend James MacLean in Keith, Banffshire, graduated MA from Marischal College in 1821, later a surgeon in the Service of the East India Company. [MCA]

MCLEAN, LACHLAN, a merchant in Danzig, Prussia, was admitted as a burgess of Banff in 1786. [BBR]

MCLEAN, WILLIAM, in Aberdeenshire, graduated MD from King's College, Aberdeen, on 30 July 1846. [KCA]

MCLEOD, ALEXANDER, formerly in the service of the East India Company, later in Fraserburgh, Aberdeenshire, testament 1793 Comm. Aberdeen. [NRS]

MCLEOD, ENEAS, a surgeon, son of Alexander McLeod in Old Deer, Aberdeenshire, died in Clarendon, Jamaica, in June 1804. [SM.66.973]

MCLEOD, JOHN, a labourer and roadmaker in Backgate, Peterhead, Aberdeenshire, was accused of bigamy with Elizabeth Ewan while lawfully married to Anne Chisholm daughter of Janet Noble a widow in Inverness, in 1834. [NRS.AD14.34.271]

MCLEOD, MARGARET, daughter of John McLeod at the Mill of Auchiries, Aberdeenshire, spouse to William Thom in Fingask, Aberdeenshire, testament, 1795, Comm. Aberdeen. [NRS]

MCNAB, JOHN, born 1807, a weaver in Peterhead, Aberdeenshire, son of Duncan McNab a ropemaker, was accused of theft in 1820. [NRS.AD14.20.261]

MCPHERSON, ALEXANDER, in Garbity, graduated MD from King's College, Aberdeen, on 25 April 1840. [KCA]

MCPHERSON, DUNCAN, born 1759 in Nairn, died in Halifax, Nova Scotia, on 31 December 1837. [HJ.1.1.1838]

MCPHERSON, JOHN, in Werdfold, Aberdeenshire, testament, 1798, Comm. Aberdeen. [NRS]

MCPHERSON, ROBERT, born 1779, a weaver in Banff, died on 1 May 1834. [Banff gravestone]

MCPHERSON, THOMAS, aged between 30 and 40, a labourer in Dairnduff, Edinlillie, Moray, was accused of murder in 1824. [NRS.AD14.24.116]

MCQUEEN, ALEXANDER, born 1826, died in Melbourne, Victoria, Australia, on 24 December 1858. [Braemar gravestone, Aberdeenshire]

MCRAE, DAVID, from Nairn, graduated MA from King's College, Aberdeen, on 27 March 1800. [KCA]

MCRAE, DANIEL, a merchant in Nairn, sederunt book, 1824/1825. [NRS.CS96.165]

MCROBERT, JOHN, born 1835, died at Fill-the-cap, Marnoch, Banffshire, in February 1885, husband of Mary S. McHardie, born 1835, died in April 1875. [Marnoch gravestone]

MCWILLIAM, DONALD, farmer in Buchromb, Mortlach, Banffshire, father of George McWilliam who died in Brooklyn, New York, on 5 November 1868. [AJ.2.12.1868]

MAIR, JAMES, son of James Mair the schoolmaster in New Deer, Aberdeenshire, graduated MA from Marischal College in 1850, later a Church of Scotland minister in Canada. [MCA]

MAITLAND, BARBARA, servant to James Robertson a cooper in Peterhead, Aberdeenshire, was imprisoned in Aberdeen Tolbooth, accused of housebreaking and theft, in 1810. [NRS.JC26.1810.6]

MALCOLM, HENRY, son of William Malcolm minister of Leochel-Cushnie, Aberdeenshire, a student at Marischal College in 1840, later a writer in Dublin, Ireland. [MCA]

MALCOLM, WILLIAM, born 1800, a schoolmaster in Echt, Aberdeenshire, for 53 years, died in the Grand Central Hotel, New York, on 27 August 1871. [S.8780][AJ.20.9.1871]

MANN, JAMES, born in Elgin, Moray, on 15 December 1795, son of John Mann and his wife Janet Laing, a husbandman, emigrated to Philadelphia, Pennsylvania, in 1812, settled in Hampstead, New Hampshire, naturalised in Rockingham County, N.H., on 11 March 1833.

MANN, WILLIAM, born 1777 in Elgin, Moray, son of John Mann and his wife Janet Laing, a ship's carpenter on an East India Company ship which was wrecked off the coast of Africa, was rescued and landed in Salem, Massachusetts, in 1803, settled in Essex County. [H]

MANSFIELD, MARY RANNIE, third daughter of John Mansfield of Midmar, Aberdeenshie, died at Pau in the Pyrenees on 21 November 1825. [SM.97.127]

MANTACH, ROBERT, BD, from Rothes, Moray, graduated MA from King's College, Aberdeen, on 27 September 1840, later an Anglican clergyman in Bermuda. [KCA]

MARQUIS, ROBERT, from Banff, graduated MA from King's College, Aberdeen, on 30 March 1797. [KCA]

MARR, WILLIAM, born 1813, a blacksmith, died in Brokenfalds on 26 April 1893, husband of Jane Dawson, born 1826, died at 115 North Street, Aberchirder, on 25 September 1903. [Marnoch gravestone, Banffshire]

MARR, Mr, a teacher of Mathematics in Banff in 1844. [AOB.ii.207]

MARTIN, JAMES, born in Aberdeenshire, 'for many years a planter in Grenada', died on board the Ferrier on passage to Tobago in 1838. [AJ.13.2.1839]

MASON, ALEXANDER, formerly a mason in Hopeman, Duffus, Moray, died in the West Indies in 1820, husband of Isobel Hardy, testament, 1822, Comm. Edinburgh. [NRS]

MASSON, JAMES, a minister in Pembroke, Canada West, nephew and heir of Joseph Duncan in Elgin, Moray, who died on 30 March 1829. [NRS.S/H]

MASSON, JAMES, born 1849, son of Alexander Masson in Harthills, Kintore, Aberdeenshire, died in Berbice on 24 January 1875. [AJ.2.2.1875]

MASSON, WILLIAM, of Caldwells, Ellon, Aberdeenshire, formerly a merchant in Aberdeen, testament, 1791, Comm. Aberdeen. [NRS]

MATHER, DAVID, born 1790 in Kincardine, died at Nerepis Settlement, New Brunswick, on 7 October 1839. [NBC.12.10.1839]

MATHER, Mrs JANE, born 1770 in the Mearns, [Kincardineshire], wife of Alexander Mather, died at Nerepis, New Brunswick, on 21 April 1824. [CG.29.4.1824]

MATTHEWS, THOMAS, born 1768, son of Andrew Matthews in Greentrae, Peterhead, Aberdeenshire, a gate porter at the Careening Yard in Halifax, Nova Scotia, died 17 September 1840, probate, 1840, Halifax, N.S.

MAURICE, JAMES, a tin-worker in Troy, USA, nephew and heir of Alexander Maurice a merchant in Turriff, Aberdeenshire, who died on 6 February 1860. [NRS.S/H]

MAVOR, JOHN, born 1789, a shoemaker in Aberdour, died 26 July 1868, husband of Elizabeth Ingram, born 1794, died 3 January 1880. [Aberdour gravestone, Aberdeenshire]

MEARNS, DAVID, a shipmaster in Johnshaven, Kincardineshire, a testament, 1801, Comm. St Andrews. [NRS]

MEARNS, DAVID, a mariner in Johnshaven, Kincardineshire, a testament, 1820, Comm. St Andrews. [NRS]

MELDRUM, ALEXANDER, a brewer in New York around 1818, husband of Agnes Sim, probably from Aberdeenshire. [NRS.CS17.1.38/347]

MELLIS, ALEXANDER, son of Alexander Mellis a farmer in Gamrie, Aberdeenshire, was educated at Marischal College in 1850s, graduated MB in 1859, later in Egypt. [MCA]

MELLIS, WILLIAM, born 1812 in Huntly, Aberdeenshire, died in New York on 20 September 1864. [AJ.26.10.1864]

MEMESS, Dr ROBERT, a physician and Episcopal minister at Fetteresso, Kincardineshire, from 1753 until his death in 1815. [NRS]

MENNIE, JANET, spouse to George Herriegerrie in Colpy, Culsalmond, Aberdeenshire, testament, 1796, Comm. Aberdeen. [NRS]

MENZIES, DAVID, from Kincardine, graduated MA from King's College, Aberdeen, in March 1823, later a Free Church minister in Glasgow. [KCA]

MERCER, Major JAMES, of Auchnacant, grandfather of John Morris West in Tuscany, Italy, in 1855. [NRS.SH]

MICHIE, ROBERT, minister at Cluny, Aberdeenshire, testaments, 1794/1795, Comm. Aberdeen. [NRS]

MIDDLEMISS, WILLIAM, and his wife Jane Stewart in Grantown, Moray, parents of James Middlemiss a planter in St Vincent, British West Indies, a deed, 1821. [NRS.RD5.201.13]

MIDDLETON, GEORGE, born 1810, son of Reverend George Middleton in Midmar, Aberdeenshire, died in Jamaica on 28 September 1852. [AJ.24.11.1852]

MIDDLETON, JAMES, a dyer at Steps of Gilcomston, a benefactor of King's College, Aberdeen, on 27 July 1810. [KCA]

MILLER, JOHN, in St Vincent, son and heir of James Miller a carter in Banff, 1840. [NRS.S/H]

MILNE, ALEXANDER, in New York, later in Banff, son and heir of John Milne a carter in Banff, 1840. [NRS.S/H]

MILNE, ALEXANDER, born 8 June 1827, son of Alexander Milne and his wife Margaret Leslie Jamieson, died in New Zealand on 9 April 1894. [Fyvie gravestone, Aberdeenshire]

MILNE, ALEXANDER, son of George Milne a farmer in Inverkeithny, Aberdeenshire, a student at Marischal College in the 1820s. [KCA]

MILNE, ALEXANDER, a farm servant in St Peter Street, Peterhead, Aberdeenshire, was accused of assault and robbery in 1846. [NRS.AD14.46.5]

MILNE, ALEXANDER PANTON, in Toronto, Ontario, nephew and heir of Francis Milne a baker in Turriff, Aberdeenshire, who died on 13October 1860. [NRS.S/H]

MILN, ANDREW, a merchant, was admitted as a burgess of Banff in 1818. [BBR]

MILNE, ARCHIBALD, son of Alexander Milne of Chapeltown, Moray, was admitted as a Notary Public on 10 June 1796, died 3 October 1812. [NRS.NP2.35.335]

MILNE, FITZROY KELLY, son of James Milne a minister in McDuff, Banffshire, a student at Marischal College around 1850, later in Australia. [MCA]

MILNE, GEORGE, in Mains of Esslemont, Aberdeenshire, testament, 1795, Comm. Aberdeen. [NRS]

MILNE, HENRY, MD, born 11 May 1812 in the Mill of Boyndie, son of John and Jean Milne, was educated at King's College, Aberdeen, in 1843, and at Edinburgh University, a physician and surgeon in Banff for 30 years, died at Bridge of Allan on 27 May 1887. [Banff parish church] [Annals of Banff.i.368, ii.365][KCA]

MILNE, ISOBEL, in Middle Savock of Lonmay, Aberdeenshire, testament, 1790, Comm. Aberdeen. [NRS]

MILNE, JAMES, from the Mearns, [Kincardineshire], graduated MA from King's College, Aberdeen, on 30 March 1791. [KCA]

MILNE, JAMES, a teacher of English in Banff in 1844. [AOB.ii.207]

MILNE, JAMES, a merchant in Soumboya, was admitted as a burgess of Banff in 1835. [BBR]

MILNE, JOHN, born in Huntly, Aberdeenshire, in 1775, died at Fall River, Massachusetts, on 4 April 1857. [AJ.13.5.1857]

MILNE, MARGARET, youngest daughter of John Milne in Stonehaven, Kincardineshire, married William Jeans of the *Melbourne Argus* in Melbourne, Victoria, Australia, on 21 February 1867. [AJ.6224]

MILNE, PATRICK, sr., a merchant in Old Meldrum, Aberdeenshire, testament, 1796, Comm. Aberdeen. [NRS]

MILNE, ROBERT, born 22 April 1775, son of Reverend James Milne and his wife Jean Milne in Rhynie, Aberdeenshire, a merchant in St Domingo, died 9 September 1814. [F.6.330]

MILNE, ROBERT, born 1801, son of Hugh Milne, a gardener in Woodend Cottage, Banchory Ternan, Kincardineshire, died in Jersey City, USA, in 1872. [AJ.4.9.1872]

MILNE, ROBERT, agent in Huntly, Aberdeenshire, for the Aberdeen Bank in 1849. [POD]

MILNE, THOMAS, agent in Ellon, Aberdeenshire, For the North of Scotland Bank in 1849. [POD]

MILNE, THOMAS, son of William Milne of the New Inn, Alford, Aberdeenshire, died in New York on 9 January 1851. [AJ.15.2.1851]

MILNE, WILLIAM, son of Alexander Milne at Grandhome Mill, was apprenticed to Alexander Thomson a cooper in Aberdeen in 1790. [ACA]

MILNE, WILLIAM, born 1797, a builder in Aberchirder, Banffshire, died 1 April 1867, husband of Ann Morrison, born 1804, died 11 January 1856. [Marnoch gravestone, Banffshire]

MILNE, Mr, born in Fochabers, Moray, died in Philadelphia on 2 January 1845. [GM.NS23.223]

MINTIE, GEORGE, son of Dr George Mintie minister at Kinnethmont, Aberdeenshire, was educated at Marischal College around 1816. [MCA]

MINTO, ANDREW, born 1786, son of Alexander Minto a farmer in Kinmore, Huntly, Aberdeenshire, a merchant in Leghorn, [Livorno], Italy, for thirty years, died there on 19 January 1838. [AJ.4717]

MINTO, J., master of the Jean of Peterhead, Aberdeenshire, bound for Greenland from Peterhead on 19 March 1826, shipwrecked off Iceland on 18 April 1826. [AJ]

MITCHELL, ALEXANDER, a writer in Edinburgh, son of James Mitchell a proofman in Elgin, Moray, was admitted as a Notary Public on 11 July 1793. [NRS.NP2.35.95]

MITCHELL, ANDREW, born 3 August 1802 in Foveran, Aberdeenshire, emigrated to Australia, died in Foveran on 23 April 1878. [Foveran gravestone]

MITCHELL, ANDREW, in Hallmoss, Inverallochy, Aberdeenshire, an inventory, 1817, Comm. Aberdeen. [NRS]

MITCHELL, or WEST, ANNE, a servant of William Downie a whitefisher in Seatown of Pittullie, Pitsligo, Aberdeenshire, was accused of housebreaking and fire-raising, an outlaw and fugitive in 1800. [NRS.JC26.1800.56]

MITCHELL, DONALD, from Nairn, graduated MA from King's College, Aberdeen, on 31 March 1809, later a missionary in India. [KCA]

MITCHELL, GEORGE, a merchant in Fraserburgh, Aberdeenshire, testament 1790, inventory, 1808, Comm. Aberdeen. [NRS]

MOGGACH, JEAN, born 1794, wife of William Robertson a farmer in Easter Auchairn, Cairnie, died 12 January 1865. [Ruthven gravestone, Aberdeenshire]

MOIR, ALEXANDER, son of Alexander Moir in Cardhillock, Newhills, Aberdeenshire, was apprenticed to William Sang a baker in Aberdeen in 1793. [ACA]

MOIR, GEORGE, born 5 April 1741, was educated at Marischal College, Aberdeen, from 1755 to 1759, minister at Peterhead, Aberdeen, from 1763 until his death on 18 March 1818, husband of Martha Byres. [F.6.232]

MOIR, GEORGE, son of William Moir in Bendach, Dyce, Aberdeenshire, was apprenticed to Margaret Morice a baker in Aberdeen in 1791. [ACA]

MOIR, GEORGE, son of William Moir a minister in Fyvie, Aberdeenshire, a student in Marischal College, graduated MA in 1794. [MCA]

MOIR, GEORGE, an engineer in Detroit, Michigan, nephew and heir of Mary Morrison in Turriff, Aberdeenshire, who died on 22 January 1863. [NRS.S/H]

MOIR, JAMES, son of George Moir a farmer in Fintray, Aberdeenshire, graduated MA from Marischal College in 1848, later a Presbyterian minister in Australia. [MCA]

MOIR, JAMES, agent for the North of Scotland Bank in Portsoy, Banffshire, in 1849. [POD]

MOIR, JOHN, in Peterhead, Aberdeenshire, a letter, 1807. [NRS.CH12.30.94]

MOIR, ROBERT, emigrated from Moray to America in 1817, settled in Rockingham County, North Carolina, in 1818, was naturalised there on 27 March 1829. [NCSA.CR84.305.1/2.47]

MOIR, WILLIAM, son of John Moir a farmer at Balcairn Mill, was apprenticed to George Moir a merchant in Aberdeen in 1791. [ACA]

MOIR, WILLIAM, born 5 October 1777, son of George Moir in Cruden, Peterhead, Aberdeenshire, was educated at King's College, Aberdeen, later a writer in Edinburgh and in Trinidad. [KCA]

MONTGOMERIE, ROBERT, in the Mains of Crichie, Aberdeenshire, an inventory, 1816, Comm. Aberdeen. [NRS]

MORGAN, Mr, in the village of Lumsden, Aberdeenshire, was appointed precentor of Banff on 13 September 1841. [AOB.ii.123]

MORRICE, ALEXANDER, born 1748, died 21 December 1820, husband of Elspet Gordon, born 1748, died 22 December 1811. [Banff gravestone]

MORICE, ALEXANDER, a sailor in Stonehaven, Kincardineshire, was accused of assault and battery in 1821. [NRS.AD14.21.130]

MORISON, ALEXANDER, in the Mains of Hatton, testament, 1791, Comm. Aberdeen. [NRS]

MORISON, ALEXANDER, a square-wright in Banff, and his wife Elizabeth Garden, parents of George Morison, born 1806, died 4 December 1834. [Banff gravestone]

MORISON, ALEXANDER, of Bognie and Mountblairy, born 30 January 1802, died 1 February 1874. [St Andrew's Episcopal Church, Banff]

MORRISON, ALEXANDER, born 1826 in Turriff, Aberdeenshire, died in Kingston, St Vincent, on 1 November 1863. [AJ.9.12.1863]

MORRISON, ALEXANDER, from Edinkillie, Moray, graduated MA from King's College, Aberdeen, in March 1851, later a schoolmaster in Hamilton, Lanarkshire, and in Melbourne, Victoria, Australia. [KCA]

MORRISON, BENJAMIN, in Jamaica, son and heir of Isobel Leslie, widow of Benjamin Morrison in Muirton of Forgue, Aberdeenshire, who died on 10 July 1810, in 1813. [NRS.S/H]

MORISON, ELSPET, in Banff, testament, 1793, Comm. Aberdeen. [NRS]

MORRISON, GEORGE, from Banff, graduated MA from King's College, Aberdeen, on 30 March 1791. [KCA]

MORRISON, GEORGE, late in Tobago, 1814, son of Alexander Morrison of Bogrie who died in September 1801. [NRS.NRAS.3585/4/2/32]

MORISON, JAMES, in Pitforskie, testament, 1793, Comm. Aberdeen. [NRS]

MORRISON, JAMES, MD, born in Inverurie, Aberdeenshire, late of the East India Company, then a farmer in Alford, emigrated to Grenada in 1858, died at the Carenage, Grenada, on 2 January 1860. [AJ.8.2.1860]

MORRISON, JANE MARGARET, daughter of Alexander Morrison of Bogrie, relict of James Ogilvie of Ascruives, wife of Alexander Gordon of Grafton Plantation, St Patrick's, Tobago, in 1794. [NRS. 2971.120]

MORISON, JOHN, born 1829, son of Reverend Joseph Morison in Millseat, King Edward, Aberdeenshire, died in Rochester, New York, on 15 August 1854. [AJ.13.9.1854]

MORRISON, JOSEPH, from King Edward, [Kinneddar], Aberdeenshire, graduated MA from King's College, Aberdeen, in March 1848, later settled at the Cape of Good Hope, South Africa. [KCA]

MORISON, JOSEPH, in Banff, son and heir of John Morison in Real del Monte in Mexico, who died in July 1853. [NRS.S/H]

MORISON, MARIA CLEOPHAS, in Banff, son and heir of John Morison in Real del Monte in Mexico, who died in July 1853. [NRS.S/H]

MORISON, THOMAS, a cooper in Fraserburgh, Aberdeenshire, a testament, 1799, Comm. Aberdeen. [NRS]

MORRISON, WILLIAM, eldest son of John Morrison the factor of Craigievar, Aberdeenshire, a baker in Aberdeen later in Port Morant, Jamaica, by 1799. [NRS.CS26.909.29]

MORTIMER, GEORGE, son of George Mortimer in Kincardine O'Neil, Aberdeenshire, graduated MA from Marischal College in 1817, later schoolmaster of Midmar. [MCA]

MORTIMER, JOHN, born 1746, miller at the Mill of Cocklarichy, died May 1802, husband of Isobel McDonald, born 1742, died 11 August 1819. [Ruthven gravestone, Aberdeenshire]

MOWAT, JANET, in Burnside, Idoch, relict of John Dent a cheesemonger in County Durham, testament, 1797, Comm. Aberdeen. [NRS]

MOWAT, MARGARET, widow of Alexander Machray of Bridgefoot, Cruden, Aberdeenshire, testament, 1800, Comm. Aberdeen. [NRS]

MUNRO, ALEXANDER, was appointed the drummer of Banff on 13 October 1831, 'was required to go with his drum through the town every morning at five o'clock'. [Annals of Banff.i.355]

MUNRO, JOHN, born 1770 in Moray, died at Portuguese Cove, Nova Scotia, on 7 May 1840. [Colonial Pearl, 9.5.1840]

MUNRO, DONALD, a sailor on the Robert of Peterhead, Aberdeenshire, was whaling off Greenland or the Davis Strait in 1794. [NRS.E508.91.10]

MUNRO, JAMES, a ships carpenter in Findhorn, Moray, a sasine, 1800. [NRS.RS.Elgin.535]

MUNRO, JOHN, in Longside, Aberdeenshire, a member of the Aberdeenshire Militia in 1808. [ACA.AS.AMI.6.1.1]

MURCAR, WILLIAM, born 1767, died 27 February 1856, husband of Margaret Clark, born 1770, died 30 July 1847. [Aberdour gravestone, Aberdeenshire]

MURCHISON, Dr ALEXANDER, late in Springfield, Jamaica, a Custos Vere and Assemblyman there, died in Elgin, Moray, on 10 October 1845. [GM.NS24.663]

MURCHISON, JOHN HENRY, eldest son of Alexander Murchison, from Elgin, Moray, late in Springfield, Jamaica, married Louis Husey, in London on 5 August 1852. [GM.NS38.411]

MURDOCH, ALEXANDER, son of Robert Murdoch a merchant in Elgin, was admitted as a burgess of Elgin, Moray, in 1792. [EBR]

MURDOCH, ALEXANDER, teacher of Writing and Arithmetic in Banff in 1829. [AOB.ii.206]

MURDOCH, JOHN, from Moray, graduated MA from King's College, Aberdeen, on 30 March 1797. [KCA]

MURISON, GEORGE, a weaver in Fraserburgh, Aberdeenshire, was accused of mobbing and rioting there in 1813. [NRS.AD4.13.88]

MURPHY, or ANDERSON, ISOBEL, a servant in Coldham, Rothiemay, Aberdeenshire, a thief who was sentenced to transportation to the colonies for seven years, at Aberdeen in May 1811. [SM.83.5.394]

MURRAY, ELLIS, was elected precentor of Banff in 1848. [AOB.ii.133]

MURRAY, GEORGE, born 1720, a quarrier, died in 1806. [Banff gravestone]

MURRAY, GEORGE FERGUSON, a merchant in Racine, Wisconsin, son and heir of John Murray in Ballus, Mintlaw, Aberdeenshire, who died on 7 May 1856. [NRS.S/H]

MURRAY, JAMES, a writer in Nairn, 1821. [NRS.CS37.2]

MURRAY, JOHN, from Banff, graduated MA from King's College, Aberdeen, on 27 March 1795. [KCA]

MURRAY, JOHN, sometime in Demerara, lately in Portsoy, Banffshire, testament, 1795, Comm. Aberdeen. [NRS]

MURRAY, PATRICK, at Ardiffery of Cruden, Aberdeenshire, an inventory, 1816. Comm. Aberdeen. [NRS]

MURRAY, WILLIAM, an apprentice on the Robert of Peterhead, Aberdeenshire, whaling off Greenland or the Davis Strait in 1791. [NRS.E508.91.8]

NAPIER, JOHN, born 3 November 1788 in Bervie, Kincardineshire, emigrated to America in 1815, a merchant in New York from 1817 until 1859, died in Brooklyn, N.Y., on 23 June 1879. [ANY]

NICHOLSON, JEAN, a servant to William Forrest in the Mains of Ludquharn, Longside, Aberdeenshire, a prisoner in Aberdeen Tolbooth, was banished from Scotland on 26 April 1799. [NRS.JC11.43]

NICOL, ANDREW, son of James Nicol in Banff, a student at Marischal College in 1830s, later a coffee planter in Ceylon. [MCA]

NICOL, GILBERT, master of the sloop Isabella of Gardenstown, Aberdeenshire, 1790. [AJ.2193]

NICOLL, JAMES, a shipmaster in Gardenstown, Banffshire, an inventory, 1805, Comm. Aberdeen. [NRS]

NICOL, JAMES, an elder of the parish of Banff in 1834. [AOB.ii.116]

NICOL, JEAN, wife of John Still a butcher in Fraserburgh, Aberdeenshire, was accused of mobbing and rioting there in 1813. [NRS.AD4.13.88]

NICOL, WILLIAM, born 1770, a weaver in Banff, died 11 April 1854, wife of Magdalen Alexander, born 1771, died 14 June 1843, parents of Duncan Nicol a saddler in Montrose, Angus. [Banff gravestone]

NICOLL, WILLIAM, a shipmaster in Gardenstown, Banffshire, later in Peterhead, Aberdeenshire, an inventory, 1812. [NRS]

NICOLSON, GEORGE, and Jane Stephen, both from Longside, Aberdeenshire, were married in Fraserburgh, Aberdeenshire, on 1 March 1794. [NRS.CH12.32.2]

NISBET, RALPH COMPTON, of Mainhouse, Roxburghshire, for 43 years a merchant in Banff, died at Mainhouse on 2 November 1863, buried in Banff. [St Andrew's Episcopal Church, Banff]

NOBLE, or SHANKY, ALEXANDER, in Fraserburgh, Aberdeenshire, was accused of mobbing and rioting there in 1813. [NRS.AD4.13.88]

NOBLE, ALEXANDER, a pilot and fisher in Fraserburgh, Aberdeenshire, was accused of mobbing and rioting there in 1813. [NRS.AD4.13.88]

NOBLE, ALEXANDER, the younger, were, in Fraserburgh, Aberdeenshire, was accused of mobbing and rioting there in 1813. [NRS.AD4.13.88]

NOBLE, CHRISTIAN, daughter of Andrew Noble a fisher on the Shore, Fraserburgh, Aberdeenshire, was accused of mobbing and rioting there in 1813. [NRS.AD4.13.88]

NOBLE, JAMES, son of Charles Noble an innkeeper in Old Deer, Aberdeenshire, a student at Marischal College, graduate MA in 1818, later minister at St Madoes, Perthshire. [MCA]

NOBLE, Mrs MARGARET, wife of Alexander Noble in Fraserburgh, Aberdeenshire, was accused of mobbing and rioting there in 1813. [NRS.AD4.13.88]

NOBLE, Mrs, born 1785, relict of James Noble in Stewartsfield, Old Deer, Aberdeenshire, later in Amherstburg, died at the residence of her son-in-law, Alexander Bartlet in Winison, Canada West, on 25 July 1861. [AJ.5928]

NORIE, JAMES, in Truro, Nova Scotia, four letters to George Duncan in Elgin, Moray, 1833-1842. [AUL.mss3015]

NORTON, CHRISTOPHER, a gentleman from Reading, Berkshire, residing in Tomley, Aberdeenshire, testament, 1800, Comm. Aberdeen. [NRS]

OFFICER, ALEXANDER MURRAY, in Stonehaven, Kincardineshire, graduated MD from King's College, Aberdeen, on 6 November 1843. [KCA]

OFFICER, JOHN, son of George Officer a merchant in Fraserburgh, Aberdeenshire, settled in Australia before 1859. [NRS.S/H]

OFFICER, ROBERT, son of Robert Officer in Jacksbank, Glenbervie, Kincardineshire, graduated MA from Marischal College in 1818, later Speaker of the Assembly in Tasmania, Australia. [MCA]

OGG, CHARLES, born 10 April 1832 in Banchory Ternan, Kincardineshire, son of Reverend Charles Ogg, graduated MA from King's College, Aberdeen, in March 1851, later a minister in New Brunswick in 1861, later in New Zealand, from 1872 to 1903, died 21 August 1905. [KCA][F.7.605]

OGILVIE, ALEXANDER, in Tochineal or Cullen, Banffshire, testament, 1798, Comm. Aberdeen. [NRS]

OGILVIE, GEORGE, born 1748, son of Alexander Ogilvie of Auchiries Aberdeenshire, and his wife Mary Cumine, settled in South Carolina and Georgia as a planter in 1774, a Loyalist who returned to Scotland, was appointed Customs Controller of Aberdeen, died in 1801. [AUL.ms2740] [TNA.AO12.51.227, etc]

OGILVIE, or DUFF, Mrs ISOBEL, in MacDuff, Banffshire, testament, 1798, Comm. Aberdeen. [NRS]

OGILVIE, JAMES, born 1772, a vintner in Banff, died 3 October 1818, husband of Mary Wood, born 1764, died 25 April 1848, parents of Alexander Ogilvie, born 1817, died in Kandy, Ceylon, on 26 September 1876. [Banff gravestone]

OGILVIE, JOHN, son of Reverend John Ogilvie in Midmar, Aberdeenshire, was apprenticed to William Michie a wright in Aberdeen in 1792. [ACA]

OGILVIE, Mrs JOHN, daughter of Alexander Morrison of Bogie, married Alexander Gordon from Tobago, at Frendraught on 25 February 1794. [SM.56.178]

OGILVIE, JOHN, from Keith, Banffshire, a teacher of Arithmetic in Banff from 1838 to 1841. [AOB.ii.207]

OGILVIE, PATRICK, born 12 September 1774, son of John Ogilvie in Midmar, Aberdeenshire, was educated at King's College, Aberdeen, from 1787 to 1791, a surgeon in St Domingo. [KCA]

OGILVIE, WILLIAM, from Banff, graduated MA from King's College, berdeen, in March 1828, later a schoolmaster in Dyke. [KCA]

OLIPHANT, MARGARET, in Knaven, Aberdeenshire, relict of Andrew Crichton in Fyvie, Aberdeenshire, testament, 1790, Comm. Aberdeen. [NRS]

ORD, JOHN, from Moray, graduated MA from King's College, Aberdeen, on 30 March 1790. [KCA]

ORR, PATRICK, a writer in Edinburgh, son of Patrick Orr in Kincardineshire, was admitted as a Notary Public on 1 June 1798. [NRS.NP2.36.177]

OSWALD, CATHERINE WHYTE, daughter of James Oswald the Superintendent of Inland Revenue in Elgin, Moray, married John Collie, a planter on Perseverance Estate, Couva, Trinidad, on 10 December 1860, she died there on 18 September 1863. [S.1743/2600]

PAGE, JAMES, a teacher in Peterhead, Aberdeenshire, cousin and heir of Helenus Page a millwright in Jamaica, 1837. [NRS.S/H]

PANTON, JOSEPH A., son of John Panton a farmer in Turriff, Aberdeenshire, a student at Marischal College in 1840s, the first Metropolitan police magistrate of Melbourne, Victoria, Australia. [MCA]

PARK, GEORGE, born 3 November 1777, in Dunnottar, Kincardineshire, son of William Park and his wife Rebecca Middleton, died in Guadaloupe, French West Indies, in 1807. [Fetteresso gravestone, Kincardineshire]

PATERSON, ALEXANDER, born 1762, a shipmaster in Macduff, Banffshire, died 25 September 1832, husband of Hellen Wilson, born 1762, died 20 December 1851. [Banff gravestone]

PATERSON, GEORGE, in Peterhead, Aberdeenshire, testament, 1805, Comm. Aberdeen. [NRS]

PATERSON, ISOBEL, in New Pitsligo, Aberdeenshire, testament, 1818, Comm. Aberdeen. [NRS]

PATERSON, JAMES, born 1745, second son of Reverend John Paterson and his wife Jean Turing, a physician who died in Jamaica on 25 April 1798. [Coull gravestone, Aberdeenshire]

PATERSON, JAMES, from Moray, graduated MA from King's College, Aberdeen, on 29 March 1798, later a minister at Birnie, Moray. [KCA]

PATERSON, JAMES, son of Reverend Paterson in Midmar, Aberdeenshire, died in Port Dover, Upper Canada, on 15 August 1849. [AJ.5307]

PATERSON, JOHN, a printer, was ordained as an elder in Banff on 21 March 1841. [AOB.ii.122]

PATTERSON, ..., master of the <u>Janet of MacDuff,</u> Banffshire, trading between Aberdeen and Fraserburgh in 1790. [AJ.2237]

PATON, GEORGE, son of Peter Paton a merchant in Fraserburgh, Aberdeenshire, graduated MA from Marischal College in 1831, later Deputy Inspector General of the East India Company. [MCA]

PATTILLO, ROBERT ALEXANDER, born 17 January 1740 in Huntly, Aberdeenshire, settled in Nova Scotia, died in Chester, N.S., on 31 December 1833.

PAUL, ALEXANDER, born 1826, son of Alexander Paul and his wife Jean Moncur, died in Lyndoch Valley, South Australia, on 10 August 1859. [Fetteresso gravestone, Kincardineshire]

PAUL, JOHN, son of John Paul a farmer in Dyce, Aberdeenshire, a student at Marischal College around 1820, later a Major of the British Army who fought in the Canadian Rebellion 1836-1837, afterwards was a clerk of works in Weston, Canada. [MCA]

PAULL, JOHN ALEXANDER, born 1842 son of George Paul of Newseat, died on Calder Estate, St Vincent, on 30 April 1868. [AJ.3.6.1868]

PAUL, JOHN, MD, from Elgin, Moray, graduated MA from King's College, Aberdeen, in March 1845, later in the Service of the East India Company. [KCA]

PAUL, WILLIAM, born 1769, farmer in Lethenty, died 8 April 1812, husband of Rachel Weir, born 1767, died 22 November 1866. [Daviot gravestone]

PEATTIE, JOHN, from Leuchars, Fife, a teacher of mathematics in Banff in 1846. [AOB.ii.207]

PENNY, ANDREW, was baptised in Birse, Aberdeenshire, on 17 May 1831, son of William Penny, jumped ship at Arica, Chile, in 1853, later was owner of the San Jose silver mine at Oruro, Bolivia, died there in 1890. [AFHS.74.37]

PEACOCK, WILLIAM, master of the Robert of Peterhead, Aberdeenshire, was whaling off Greenland or the Davis Strait in 1794. [NRS.E508.94.10]

PETERKIN, ALEXANDER, of Chatham, Jamaica, and of Greshope, Moray, died in Cheltenham, Gloucestershire, in 1818. [BM.2.610]

PETERKIN, WILLIAM, from Moray, graduated MA from King's College, Aberdeen, on 28 March 1799. [KCA]; a teacher of English in Banff in 1805. [AOB.ii.206]

PETRIE, GEORGE, a stove manufacturer in New York, son and heir of James Petrie a tinsmith in Forres, Moray, 1837. [NES.S/H]

PETRIE, JOHN, born 1741, tenant in Stewartfield, died 22 March 1825, husband of Elisabeth Anderson, born 1749, died 8 May 1825. [New Deer gravestone, Aberdeenshire]

PETRIE, J., agent of the North of Scotland Bank in Dufftown in 1849. [POD]

PHILIPS, ALEXANDER born 1754 in Elgin, Moray, died in Halifax, Nova Scotia, on 27 December 1837. [AR.30.12.1837]

PHILIP, JAMES, in Ontario, brother and heir of Jane Philip a teacher in Keith Hall, Aberdeenshire, who died on 30 March 1850. [NRS.S/H]

PHILIP, WILLIAM, in Muirton of Barra, Aberdeenshire, testament, 1790, Comm. Aberdeen. [NRS]

PHILIP, WILLIAM MARSHALL, son of Thomas Philip a teacher in Grange, Banffshire, a student at Marischal College in 1850s, later a minister in Canada. [MCA]

PIRIE, ALEXANDER, late merchant in Banff, left funds to provide a free school in the Seatown of Banff, 20 October 1805. [AOB.II.114]

PIRIE, GEORGE, born 9 April 1798 in Cairnie, Aberdeenshire, son of John Pirie and his wife Christina Robertson, was educated at King's College, Aberdeen, in 1817, a surgeon in America. [KCA]

PIRIE, JANET, in Cloak, testament, 1790, Comm. Aberdeen. [NRS]

PIRIE, JOHN, born 1759, merchant in Ruthven, died 27 May 1818, husband of Christian Richardson, born 1763, died 26 June 1803, parents of James Pirie, [1792-1801], George Pirie, MD, born 1800, died in Grenada in 1828, James Pirie, born 1801, died in Boston, Massachusetts in 1829, and James Pirie, born 1797, farmer at Little Daugh, died 1871. [Ruthven gravestone]

PIRIE, WILLIAM, a servant to Harry Watson in Mill of Fintray, Aberdeenshire, testament, 1797, Comm. Aberdeen. [NRS]

PITTENDREICH, MARY, at Nether Kinmundy, Longside, daughter of James Pittendreich a gardener or nurseryman in Longside, testament, 1793, Comm. Aberdeen. [NRS]

PORTER, WILLIAM, MA, born 1815, son of Francis Porter a farmer in Auchintender, Forgue, Aberdeenshire, graduated MA from King's College, Aberdeen, in March 1835, died at Mount Pleasant, St Vincent, on 22 February 1847. [AJ.5178][KCA]

PRESSLEY, Reverend CHARLES, son of Charles Pressley a merchant in Fraserburgh, graduated MA from Marischal College in 1819, later an Episcopalian minister in Fraserburgh, Aberdeenshire, a letter to Bishop Walker in 1834. [MCA] [NRS.CH12.14.94]

PRINGLE, JOHN, an elder of the parish of Banff in 1834. [AOB.ii.116]

PURSE, JOHN, born 12 December 1732 in Elgin, Moray, son of Alexander Purse, a tailor, and his wife Isabel Blenshel, a merchant in Quebec by 1762, heir to his father Alexander Purse a tailor in Elgin in 1794, also grandson and heir of William Blanchil a tailor in Elgin, Moray, in 1794, died in Quebec on 8 April 1803. [NRS.S/H][DCB]

PYPER, WILLIAM, a stocking maker at the Brae of Pitfoddels, Aberdeenshire, testament, 1791, Comm. Aberdeen. [NRS]

RAE, JOHN E., from Edinburgh, a teacher of English in Banff 1849-1851. [AOB.ii.207]

RAE, GEORGE, in America, grandson and heir of George Rae a blacksmith in Rosehearty, Aberdeenshire, who died in 1825. [NRS.S/H]

RAE, JOHN, agent in Ellon, Aberdeenshire, for the Aberdeen Town and County Bank in 1849. [POD]

RAEBURN, Mrs ANNE, born 1847, wife of Alexander Raeburn from Cartiehaugh, Old Deer, Aberdeenshire, died in Stamford, Connecticut, on 22 February 1869. [AJ.17.3.1869]

RAEBURN, JAMES, born 1822, son of Reverend Gordon Raeburn schoolmaster at Keig, Aberdeenshire, manager of Lavington's Estate in Antigua, died on 17 June 1851. [AJ.5399]

RAMAGE, JOHN, born 1798, accountant of the National Bank in Banff, died 24 February 1832, husband of Lilias Hardie, born 1797, died 24 February 1860. [Banff gravestone]

RAMSAY, ALEXANDER, a merchant in Rosehearty, Aberdeenshire, and his sister Barbara Ramsay there, testament, 1792, Comm. Aberdeen. [NRS]

RAMSAY, JOHN, Major of the Company of the Peterhead Company of Volunteers, Aberdeenshire, letters, 1798-1801. [NRS.GD44.47.45.4]

RANKEN, WILLIAM, born 1769, a square-wright in Fraserburgh, Aberdeenshire, died 31 January 1855, husband of May Watson, born 1773, died 16 February 1853. [Fraserburgh Kirkton gravestone]

RANKIN, WILLIAM, born in Aberdeenshire, a schoolteacher who died in Middleton, Galt, Upper Canada, on 6 December 1846. [AJ.5172]

RANKIN, WILLIAM, from Fraserburgh, Aberdeenshire, died in New York on 22 June 1853. [AJ.20.7.1853]

RANNIE, Reverend WILLIAM, in Fochabers, Moray, married Catherine Matilda Evans, daughter of Charles Evans in Woolwich, in Corsaitly on 1 December 1825. [SM.97.126]

RAY, JOHN, in Findhorn, master of the Buxar, testament, 1804, Comm. Moray. [NRS]

REA, JAMES, born 1809 in Moray, died in Halifax, Nova Scotia, on 22 April 1834. [AR.28.4.1834]

REID, A., agent in Fochabers, Moray, for the Aberdeen Bank in 1849. [POD]

REID, ALEXANDER, youngest son of James Reid in Ardoch, Banffshire, an overseer of Tryall Estate, Jamaica, died on Orchard Estate, Jamaica, on 3 November 1827. [S.853.170]

REID, ALEXANDER, son of Alexander Reid in the Mains of Barra, Aberdeenshire, was apprenticed to James Finnie a wright in Aberdeen, in 1792. [ACA]

REID, ALEXANDER, an elder of the parish of Banff in 1834. [AOB.ii.116]

REID, GEORGE, son of James Reid of Ardoch, Banffshire, died on Bellfield Estate, Demerara, on 26 July 1819. [S.145.19]

REID, ISABEL, in Upper Drumalachy, testament, 1808, Comm. Aberdeen. [NRS]

REID, JAMES, a skipper in Fraserburgh, inventory, 1808, Comm. Aberdeen. [NRS]

REID, JAMES, in Tornaveen, Aberdeenshire, testament, 1808, Comm. Aberdeen. [NRS]

REID, JAMES, a Lieutenant of the Royal Navy, eldest son of James Reid in Fraserburgh, Aberdeenshire, died in Buenos Ayres, Argentina, on 23 December 1819. [S.4.171]

REID, JAMES, in Louisiana, grandson and heir of William Reida merchant in Lossiemouth, Moray, who died on 30 May 1832. [NRS.S/H]

REID, JAMES, born 1758, died 7 November 1836, husband of Anne Duff Forbes born 1756, died 6 May 1838. [Banff gravestone]

REID, JAMES, in Aberdeenshire, graduated MD from King's College, Aberdeen, on 5 August 1848. [KCA]

REID, JOHN, a shipmaster in Fraserburgh, Aberdeenshire, inventory and testament, 1808, Comm. Aberdeen. [NRS]

REID, JOHN, from Moray, graduated MA from King's College, Aberdeen, on 30 March 1791. [KCA]

REID, JOHN, a skipper in Lossiemouth, testament, 1820, Comm. Moray. [NRS]

REID, JOHN, born 1791, son of James Reid in Ardoch, Banffshire, a surgeon of the 50th Regiment, died in Sydney, New South Wales, Australia, in January 1840. [AJ.4827]

REID, JOHN, born 1793, son of George Reid a mason in Banff and his wife Mary Duffus, a seaman who died at sea near Valparaiso, Chile, on 3 April 1824.

REID, JOSEPH, from Rothiemay, Banffshire, graduated MA from King's College, Aberdeen, in March 1839, later a government teacher at the Cape of Good Hope, South Africa. [KCA]

REID, MARGARET, in Fraserburgh, Aberdeenshire, a testament, 1811, Comm. Aberdeen. [NRS]

REID, MARGARET ANNE, in Westminster, Canada, daughter and heir of William Reid a merchant in Llanbryde, Moray, who died on 12 May 1855. [NRS.S/H]

REID, MARY, was admitted as a burgess of Banff in 1800. [BBR]

REID, MARY, daughter of James Reid a shipowner in Fraserburgh, Aberdeenshire, married John J. J. Alexander from St Lucia, British West Indies, in Bath, England, on 31 August 1813. [SM.75]

REID, PETER, from Fochabers, Moray, son of Peter Reid a coachman in Aberdeen, a student at Marischal College in 1850s, later a chemist in Wiesbaden, Germany. [MCA]

REID, THOMAS, a master of the Royal Navy in Halifax, Nova Scotia, later in Peterhead, Aberdeenshire, inventory and testament, 1804, Comm. Aberdeen. [NRS]

REID, WILLIAM, from Kildrummy, Aberdeenshire, graduated MA from King's College, Aberdeen, in March 1834, later a Free Church minister in Toronto, Canada. [KCA]

REID, WILLIAM, a merchant in New Deer, Aberdeenshire, testament, 1790, Comm. Aberdeen. [NRS]

REID, WILLIAM, a shipmaster in Peterhead, Aberdeenshire, testament, 1792, Comm. Aberdeen. [NRS]

REID, WILLIAM, born 1840, eldest son of Arthur Reid a banker in Fochabers, Moray, died at his residence in Russell Street, Dunedin, New Zealand, on 31 May 1884. [S.12812]

RETTIE, JANET, in Broomhill, New Deer, Aberdeenshire, testament, 1799, Comm. Aberdeen. [NRS]

RIACH, ALEXANDER, teacher of English in Banff in 1833. [AOB.ii.207]

RIACH, ALEXANDER FRIDGE, in New York, son and heir of Peter Riach a merchant in Forres, Moray, who died on 30 August 1864. [NRS.S/G]

RIACH, PETER, in Bellamore, testament, 1792, Comm. Aberdeen. [NRS]

RIDDOCH, GEORGE, from Banff, graduated MA from King's College, Aberdeen, on 28 March 1799. [KCA]

RIDGEWELL, WILLIAM, born 1830 in Banffshire, emigrated in1851, declared his intention to naturalise in Norfolk County Circuit Court, Virginia, on 15 November 1856.

RITCHIE, GEORGE, formerly in Barbados, later in Demerara, died 1790, brother of John Ritchie a merchant in Elgin, Moray, testament, 1791, Comm. Edinburgh. [NRS]

RITCHIE, JAMES, a sailor on the <u>Hope of Stonehaven,</u> Kincardineshire, was accused of assault and battery in 1821. [NRS.AD14.21.130]

RITCHIE, JAMES, a blacksmith in Kildrummie, Nairn, a victim of theft in 1825. [NRS.AD14.25.229]

RITCHIE, MARGARET, wife of ….. Reid in Fraserburgh, Aberdeenshire, testament, 1811, Comm. Aberdeen. [NRS]

RITCHIE, SOPHIA, widow of John Fraser a shipmaster in Fraserburgh, Aberdeenshire, testament, 1811, Comm. Aberdeen. [NRS]

RITCHIE, WILLIAM, an engineer from Aberdeenshire, who was killed on the New Jersey railway on 12 March 1860. [AJ.11.4.1860]

ROBB, Mrs ISABELLA, in Nether Kinmundy, Aberdeenshire, testament, 1792, Comm. Aberdeen. [NRS]

ROBB, JOHN, born 1793 in Boharm, Banffshire, died in Halifax, Nova Scotia, on 19 March 1842. [HJ.21.3.1842]

ROBERTSON, ALEXANDER, a merchant in Portsoy, Banffshire, testament, 1791, Comm. Aberdeen. [NRS]

ROBERTSON, ALEXANDER, of Blackchambers, testament, 1793, Comm. Aberdeen. [NRS]

ROBERTSON, ALEXANDER, a bank manager in London, son and heir of James Robertson formerly in Jamaica, later in Elgin, Moray, who died on 31 July 1816. [NRS.S/H]

ROBERTSON, ALEXANDER, late farmer in Craigairn, Kemnay, Aberdeenshire, died at Long Point, Montreal, Quebec, on 14 May 1847. [AJ.5192]

ROBERTSON, ALEXANDER, a planter in Tobago, died 16 November 1814, possibly from Abernethy, testament, 1817, Comm. Edinburgh. [NRS]

ROBERTSON, ALEXANDER, son of Robert Robertson of Boddam, Peterhead, Aberdeenshire, was a student at Marischal College around 1817, later a baker in Peterhead. [MCA]

ROBERTSON, ARCHIBALD, born 1834, late of Woodside, died on Broadway, New York, on 24 August 1856. [AJ.5670]

ROBERTSON, CHARLES, at Point Livy, Quebec, brother and heir of Mary Robertson in Ruthrieston, Aberdeenshire, who died on 21 May 1861. [NRS.S/H]

ROBERTSON, CHRISTINE, in Nairn, 1821. [NRS.CS44.1.12]

ROBERTSON, FRANCIS, born 1747 in Aberdeenshire, a lawyer who emigrated to South Carolina before 1789, died in Charleston, S.C., on October 1819. [GM.90.281][AJ.3795][S.4.193]

ROBERTSON, GEORGE, son of Patrick Robertson a merchant in Huntly, Aberdeenshire, graduated MA from Marischal College in 1817, later a schoolmaster in Aberdeen. [MCA]

ROBERTSON, GEORGE, agent in Elgin, Moray, for the North of Scotland Bank in 1849. [POD]

ROBERTSON, HARRY, of Newton, formerly in Havannah, Cuba, a sasine, 6 October 1838. [NRS.RS.Nairn.4/117]

ROBERTSON, ISAAC, born 1780, formerly a farmer in Cairney, Aberdeenshire, died in Montreal, Quebec, on 18 October 1837. [AJ.4696]

ROBERTSON, JAMES, born 1736 in Banffshire, emigrated to New Brunswick in 1764, a master cooper, died in Bathurst, New Brunswick, on 29 October 1834. [NBC.29.11.1834]

ROBERTSON, JAMES, from Banff, graduated MA from King's College, Aberdeen, on 29 March 1793. [KCA]

ROBERTSON, JAMES, a merchant in Rosehearty, Aberdeenshire, testament, 1794, Comm. Aberdeen. [NRS]

ROBERTSON, JAMES, jr., born 1793 in Huntly, Aberdeenshire, emigrated to New Brunswick in 1815, editor of the *New Brunswick Courier*, died in St John, N.B., on 11 March 1830. [CG.17.3.1830]

ROBERTSON, JAMES, a teacher of English in Banff from 1827 to 1833. [AOB.ii.206]

ROBERTSON, JAMES F., son of William Robertson of Hazlehead, Aberdeenshire, was educated at Marischal College in 1840s, later a Colonel of the Bombay Staff Corps. [MCA]

ROBERTSON, JAMES, from Marnoch, Banffshire, graduated MA in March 1843, also MD from King's College, Aberdeen, on 6 April 1847, settled in Melbourne, Victoria, Australia. [KCA]

ROBERTSON, JOSEPH, eldest son of Mr Robertson in Elgin, Moray, died in Jamaica on 26 November 1807. [SM.70.398]

ROBERTSON, J., agent in Huntly, Aberdeenshire, for the North of Scotland Banking Company in 1849. [POD]

ROBERTSON, LEWIS, born 1816, son of Lewis Robertson and his wife Jane Inkson, died in Australia on 25 January 1847. [Knockando gravestone, Banffshire]

ROBERTSON, RACHEL, widow of William White in Aberdeen, sister and heir of Adam Topp in Jamaica, who died on 26 August 1868. [NRS.S/H]

ROBERTSON, ROBERT, son of Thomas Robertson a merchant in Peterhead, Aberdeenshire, a writer there, was admitted as a Notary Public on 10 December 1791. [NRS.NP2.34.305]

ROBERTSON, WILLIAM, in Inver of Monymusk, Aberdeenshire, testament, 1796, Comm. Aberdeen. [NRS]

ROBERTSON, WILLIAM, [1787-1874], and his wife Mary Reith, [1790-1877], in Banchory Devenick, Kincardineshire, parents of James Robertson who settled in Australia before 1877. [Banchory Devenick gravestone]

ROBERTSON, WILLIAM, from Moray, graduated MA at King's College, Aberdeen, a minister of the Dutch Reformed Church, died in 1879. [F.7.564]

ROBERTSON, W. T., late Judge of Burdwan, in the Bengal Civil Service, eldest son of Colin Robertson in Elgin, Moray, died at the Cape of Good Hope, South Africa, on 27 April 1835. [AJ.4569]

ROBINSON, ALEXANDER, Naval Officer of Kingston, Jamaica, third son of James Robinson in Bishop Mill, Moray, died in Port Royal Harbour, Jamaica, on 19 September 1791. [SM.53.568]

ROGER, ALEXANDER, son of James Roger a merchant in Rhynie, Aberdeenshire, was educated at Marischal College, Aberdeen, in 1853, a schoolmaster in New Zealand. [MCA]

ROGER, WALTER, son of Reverend J. Roger in Kincardine O'Neil, Aberdeenshire, Deputy Sheriff of New South Wales, Australia, died in Sydney in 1833. [AJ.4462]

ROSE, ALEXANDER, from Moray, graduated MA from King's College, Aberdeen, on 30 March 1791. [KCA]

ROSE, ANDREW, seventh son of William Rose in Gask, Aberdeenshire, Secretary to the Council of St Vincent, died at Mount Rose, St Vincent, on 19 February 1822. [BM.11.629]

ROSE, JAMES, of Geddes, Nairnshire, graduated MA from King's College, Aberdeen, on 29 March 1793. [KCA]

ROSE, JOHN, from Banff, graduated MA from King's College, Aberdeen, in March 1840, later a surgeon in the Royal Navy. [KCA]

ROSE, MARY, only daughter of William Baillie Rose of Rhynie, Aberdeenshire, and his wife Helen Cockburn, and Alexander MacBarnet on St Vincent, British West Indies, a marriage contract dated 1824. [NRS.RD5.282.159]

ROSE, Dr, from Nairn, a physician in Jamaica in 1808. [NRS.GD171.914]

ROSS, ALEXANDER, son of Alexander Ross in Strathdon, Aberdeenshire, was apprenticed to William Leys a cooper in Aberdeen, in 1791. [ACA]

ROSS, ALEXANDER IRVINE, in Fraserburgh, Aberdeenshire, a victim of rioting in 1813. [NRS.AD4.13.88]

ROSS, ANDREW, agent for the Aberdeen Bank in Tarland, Aberdeenshire, in 1849. [POD]

ROSS, GEORGE, a carrier in Turriff, Aberdeenshire, father of James Ross in Balnamore, Ireland, 1839. [NRS.S/H]

ROSS, JOHN, from Moray, graduated MA from King's College, Aberdeen, on 30 March 1790. [KCA]

ROSS, GEORGE, steersman aboard the whaler Robert of Peterhead off Greenland in 1794. [NRS.E508.94.8/10]

ROSS, JAMES, son of John Leith of Arnage, a gentleman, graduated MA from Marischal College in 1830s, settled in Guelph, Canada, later a Member of the first Parliament of Canada in 1869. [MCA]

ROSS, JAMES, son of Peter Ross a farmer in Gartly, a student at Marischal College on 1830s, later a planter in Demerara. [MCA]

ROSS, JOHN, line manager aboard the whaler Robert of Peterhead off Greenland or the Davis Straits in 1791. [NRS.E508.91.8]

ROSS, JOHN, sr., a fisherman in the Seatown of Cullen, Banffshire, was to be denounced as a rebel as he had failed to come to Banff as agreed on 25 January 1810. [Annals of Banff, i.351]

ROSS, MALCOLM, a labourer at the Mains of Waterton, Ellon, Aberdeenshire, was accused of horse-stealing in 1847. [NRS.AD14.47.2212]

ROSS, THOMAS, born 1733 in Moray, died in Halifax, Nova Scotia, on 16 May 1832. [AR.19.5.1832]

ROSS, WILLIAM, born 1741, son of James Ross and his wife Agnes Dunn in the Mill of Towtie, died in Jamaica in 1798. [Fetteresso gravestone, Kincardineshire]

ROSS, WILLIAM, born 1820 in Huntly, Aberdeenshire, son of William Ross a watchmaker, was educated at Marischal College, Aberdeen, in 1840, later a minister in Australia from 1846 to 1880, died in Scotland in August 1899. [F.7.597]

ROSS, ..., master of the Adventure of Banff trading between Aberdeen and Wick in 1790. [AJ2236]

ROY, GEORGE, born 1751 in Banff, an early settler in Halifax, North America, died in Merigomish, Halifax, in 1831. [GM.101.477]

ROY, JOHN, in Laichie of Mortlach, Banffshire, testament, 1795, Comm. Aberdeen. [NRS]

RUDDACH, JOHN, a surgeon at Montego Bay, Jamaica, was admitted as a burgess of Banff in 1800. [BBR]

RUGLAN, JAMES, a weaver in Old Rayne, Aberdeenshire, testament, 1795, Comm. Aberdeen. [NRS]

RUNCIE, JOHN, born 1791, farmer in Cairnwhelp, Cairnie, died at New Mill, Keith, on 12 June 1856. [Ruthven gravestone, Aberdeenshire]

RUSSELL, ALEXANDER, of Moncoffer, Banffshire, died in Aden, Aberdeenshire, on 26 July 1831. [AJ.4360]

RUSSELL, GEORGE, a writer in Edinburgh, son of Alexander Russell of Moncoffer, Banffshire, was admitted as a Notary Public on 6 February 1794. [NRS.NP2.35.107]

RUSSELL, JAMES, born 1815, son of William Russell, 'late of California', died in 1904. [Kinnedar gravestone, Moray]

RUSSELL, THOMAS, son of Thomas Russell in Rathen, Aberdeenshire, died in Martinique, French West Indies, in July 1794. [EA.3215.254]

RUSSELL, GEORGE, son of Alexander Russell of Aden, Aberdeenshire, graduated MA from Marischal College in 1817, later a merchant in Liverpool. [MCA]

RUSSELL, THOMAS, son of Alexander Russell of Aden, Old Deer, Aberdeenshire, was educated at Marischal College around 1816, later graduated MD from Edinburgh University in 1822. [MCA]

RUSSELL, WILLIAM, in New Pitsligo, Aberdeenshire, a testament, 1812, Comm. Aberdeen. [NRS]

RUTHERFORD, JOHN, born 1764, of Cuttlehill, Ruthven, died in October 1840, husband of Helen McPherson, born 1771, died in April 1855, parents of John Rutherford, born 1803, died 1857, and Jane, born 1805, died at Rhynie in 1903. [Ruthven gravestone, Aberdeenshire]

RUXTON, ROBERT, born 1747, son of Robert Ruxton of Cairnhill, Esslemont, Aberdeenshire, married Margaret Brown from Cononsyth, Angus, emigrated to America in 1788, died in 1828.

SAMUEL, GRIZEL, born 1787, wife of Alexander Willox a harpooner in Peterhead, Aberdeenshire, was accused of housebreaking and theft in 1821. [NRS.AD14.21.256]

SANG, THOMAS, son of Robert Sang in Green Loan, Kincardine, was apprenticed to Joseph Berrie a weaver in Aberdeen in 1791. [ACA]

SANGSTER, JOHN, born 1797, farmer at Northside, Daviot, died 3 March 1874, husband of Elspet Thomson, born 1800, died 11 June 1880. [Daviot gravestone]

SANGSTER, JOHN, in Trinidad, son and heir to James Sangster in the Mains of Pitrichie, Old Meldrum, Aberdeenshire, 1808. [NRS.S/H]

SANGSTER, WILLIAM, a clerk in Montreal, grandson and heir of John Christie a feuar in Macduff, Banffshire, in 1810. [NRS.S/H]

SANGSTER, Reverend WILLIAM, born 1745, Episcopalian minister in Lonmay, Aberdeenshire, for 57 years, died there on 4 January 1826, [SM.97.255];a letter to Alexander Jolly, 1804. [NRS. CH12.8.1804]

SCORGIE, JANET, in Fraserburgh, Aberdeenshire, testament, 1796, Comm. Aberdeen. [NRS]

SCOTT, ALEXANDER, a sailor in Garmouth, Moray, father of Alexander Scott in Garmouth, a sasine 1791. [NRS.RS.Elgin.280]

SCOTT, CHARLES, son of William Scott a merchant in Peterhead, Aberdeenshire, graduated MA from Marischal College in 1819, later a minister in Natal, South Africa. [MCA]

SCOTT, JAMES, gardener at Logie, testament, 1797, Comm. Aberdeen. [NRS]

SCOTT, JAMES, born 18 February 1778, son of Archibald Scott, in Pitarrow, Fordoun, Kincardineshire, to India in 1797, a Lieutenant Colonel of the Bengal Army, died on 11 August 1820. [BA.4.35]

SCOTT, JAMES, born 1782, a physician, died in the Kirkton of Fraserburgh, Aberdeenshire, in 1831. [AJ.14.8.1832]

SCOTT, JOHN, master of the <u>Concord of Banff,</u> was wrecked near Whitby, England, in 1792. [AJ.2349]

SCOTT, JOHN, in Lumbs, testament, 1792, Comm. Aberdeen. [NRS]

SCOTT, JOHN, a merchant in Stonehaven, Kincardineshire, a bankrupt who absconded to America in 1817. [NRS.CS233.s.i.45]

SCOTT, ROBERT, from Banff, graduated MA from King's College, Aberdeen, on 27 March 1800, later a minister in Glenbucket, Aberdeenshire. [KCA]

SCOTT, WILLIAM, in the Mains of Brucklaw, testaments, 1798/1800, Comm. Aberdeen. [NRS]

SCOTT, WILLIAM, jr., a merchant in Peterhead, Aberdeenshire, testament, 1812, Comm. Aberdeen. [NRS]

SCOTT, WILLIAM, a yeoman in Wilmot, Canada, brother and heir of James Scott a farmer in Achath, Aberdeenshire, who died on 18 January 1815. [NRS.S/H]

SCOTT, Mrs, wife of Reverend James Scott from Peterhead, Aberdeenshire, died in Demerara on 12 January 1836. [AJ.4596]

SELLER, ROBERT, master of the Mary of Peterhead, Aberdeenshire, trading between Easdale and Inverness in1807. [NRS.E504.17.8]

SETON, JOHN, in Whitside of Rathven, Aberdeenshire, testament, 1791, Comm. Aberdeen. [NRS]

SETON, ALEXANDER, of Mounie, Lieutenant Colonel of the 74th Regiment of Highlanders, who was drowned, with 400 of his men, in the wreck of HMS Birkenhead near Point Danger, Cape of Good Hope, South Africa, on 26 February 1852. [Daviot gravestone]

SHAND, ALEXANDER ALLAN, son of James Shand of Turriff, Aberdeenshire, married Emmaline C. Protheroe from Kent, in Yokohama, Japan, on 15 December 1870. [AJ.6423]

SHAND, CHARLES, son of Reverend James Shand in Marykirk, Kincardineshire, was educated at Marischal College 1825-1828, was an Advocate in Edinburgh, became Chief Justice of Mauritius. [MCA]

SHAND, FRANCIS, born in Kemnay, Aberdeenshire, on 2 August 1786, second son of Reverend John Shand and his wife Margaret Dauney, was educated at King's College, Aberdeen, from 1799 to 1803, an advocate who died in Spanish Town, Jamaica, on 10 March 1827. [KCA][SAA]

SHAND, GEORGE, in Demerara, later in Aberdeen, husband of Mary Walker, testament, 1793, Comm. Aberdeen. [NRS]

SHAND, GEORGE, born in Huntly, Aberdeenshire, died of yellow fever in New Orleans, Louisiana, on 2 September 1839. [AJ.4803]

SHAND, ISABELLA, fourth daughter of James Shand in Inverurie, Aberdeenshire, married Reverend Michael Watt, in Willowbank, Otago, New Zealand, on 30 August 1866. [AJ.6210]

SHAND, JOHN, from Kincardineshire, a planter in Jamaica around 1800. [NRS.CS46.1852]

SHAND, JOHN, from Banff, graduated MA from King's College, Aberdeen, on 2 April 1804, later a schoolmaster at Oyne. [KCA]

SHAND, JOHN, son of Reverend James Shand in Marykirk, Kincardineshire, graduated MA from Marischal College in 1816, later became a Writer to the Signet in 1823. [MCA]

SHAND, JOHN, in Spanish Town, Jamaica, proprietor of the estate of Burn, Arnhall, Kincardineshire, appointed Reverend John Anderson in Bellie, Fochabers, Moray, as his attorney, in 1816. [NRS.RD5.92.619]

SHAND, JOHN, a merchant in the West Indies, died in 1825. [Fettercairn gravestone, Kincardineshire]

SHAND, ROBERT, from Aberdeenshire, a student at King's College, Aberdeen, from 1819 until 1823, a minister of the Dutch Reformed Church in South Africa from 1834, died in 1876. [F.7.564]

SHAND, WILLIAM, an estate manager in Jamaica from 1791 until 1823, later in Arnhall, Kincardineshire. [NRS.CS46.1852]; his wife died in Mamee Gulley, Jamaica, on 19 February 1826. [BM.19.765]

SHAND, WILLIAM, of Balmakewan, Kincardineshire, in Hopewell, St Ann, Jamaica, in 1825. [BM.18.779]

SHAND, Reverend WILLIAM, born 1738, died in the Manse of Lumphanan, Aberdeenshire, in January 1826. [SM.97.255]

SHAND, WILLIAM, from Mortlach, Banffshire, graduated MA from King's College, Aberdeen, in March 1843, later a teacher at the Cape of Good Hope, South Africa. [KCA]

SHARP, JAMES, from Rothes, Moray, a mason in Halifax, Nova Scotia, probate 1796, Halifax, N.S.

SHAW, DAVID, born 1758 in Aberdeenshire, a traveling Gospel preacher, died in Sussex Vale, New Brunswick, on 26 May 1838. [NBC.9.6.1838]

SHAW, ISABELLA, daughter of James Shaw of Muirton, married Henry Bridgewater from Grenada, in Forres, Moray, in 1813. [EA.5195.13]

SHAW, WILLIAM, born 1831, son of Alexander Shaw, 1790-1859, died on Carriacou, near Grenada, on 9 October 1864. [Crathie gravestone, Aberdeenshire]

SHEARER, GEORGE, born 1800, a clothier in Banff, died 28 October 1886. [Banff gravestone]

SHEARER, WILLIAM, and Eliza Hope, both from Moray, were married in Newport, Nova Scotia, on 7 May 1833. [HJ.13.5.1833]

SHEPHERD, PETER, son of Peter Shepherd a farmer in Leochel, Aberdeenshire, a student in 1850s, graduated MB from Aberdeen University in 1864, a Surgeon Major who was killed at the Battle of Isandula, South Africa, in 1879. [MCA]

SHEPHERD, THOMAS, son of Reverend Robert Shepherd in Daviot, Aberdeenshire a student at Marischal College around 1812, later a Captain of the Marine Service of the East India Company. [MCA]

SHEWAN, ALEXANDER, from St Fergus, Aberdeenshire, was educated at King's College, Aberdeen, around 1855, later a Professor in Montreal, Quebec. [KCA]

SHIER, DAVID, son of David Shier in Banff, graduated MD from Marischal College in 1841, later in Demerara. [MCA]

SHINNIE, ALEXANDER, born 1782 in Kincardineshire, a millwright in Charleston, South Carolina, naturalised there on 31 July 1831, died on 31 October 1834. [Telescope; 9.11.1834] [NARA.M1183]

SHIRRAS, ALEXANDER, born 1753 in Old Deer, Aberdeenshire, a merchant in Charleston, South Carolina, from around 1781 until his death on 20 October 1811. [St Michael's gravestone, Charleston, S.C.]

SHIRRAS, BARBARA, relict of Robert Brebner in Hilltown, testament, 1799, Comm. Aberdeen. [NRS]

SHIRREFFS, LAUDERDALE, born 1837, died in Demerara in 1854. [Banchory Ternan gravestone, Aberdeenshire]

SHIVAS, ANDREW, a vintner in Peterhead, Aberdeen, testament, 1795, Comm. Aberdeen. [NRS]

SHORT, ANN, in Fraserburgh, Aberdeenshire, was accused of mobbing and rioting there in 1813. [NRS.AD4.13.88]

SHURIE, WILLIAM, a mariner in Peterhead, inventory, 1818, Comm. Aberdeen. [NRS]

SIM, ANDREW, born in Ellon, Aberdeenshire, died on Plantation Garden of Eden, Demerara, on 7 August 1821. [S.5.257][BM.10.609]

SIM, JAMES, born 11 November 1759 in Banff, late of St Vincent, died 27 May 1825, husband of Elizabeth McKilligan, born 22 November

1761 in Banff, died 24 March 1826, parents of Elizabeth born 13 May 1805, died 27 November 1810, Barbara born 1801, died 31 January 1885, and James George Sim MD, of the East India Company, born in Banff on 4 March 1804, died in Singapore on 10 September 1830. [Banff gravestone]

SIM, JAMES, a fisher in Pitsligo, inventory, 1821, Comm. Aberdeen. [NRS]

SIM, JOHN, born 1744, late of Antigua, died 29 November 1807, his wife Mary Stephen, born 1756, died 29 February 1847. [Banff gravestone]

SIM, WILLIAM, [1821-1893], and his wife Mary Stewart, [1824-1908], in Braemar, Aberdeenshire, parents of George C. Sim, born 1850, settled in California by 1878, died in San Francisco in 1906. [Braemar gravestone] [NRS.GD1.756.2]

SIME, ALEXANDER, born 1845, son of Alexander Sime, a farmer in Ringorm, and his wife Margaret Donaldson, died in Warnambool, Australia, on 24 June 1886. [Knockando gravestone, Banffshire]

SIME, LEWIS, born 1848, son of Alexander Sime a farmer in Ringorm and his wife Margaret Donaldson, died in St Thomas, Canada, on 15 March 1871. [Knockando gravestone, Banffshire]

SIMPSON, ALEXANDER FRASER, second son of Reverend Alexander Simpson in Fraserburgh, Aberdeenshire, was educated at Marischal College, Aberdeen, from 1816 until 1820, died in Vere, Jamaica, on 24 July 1834. [AJ.4540][MCA]

SIMPSON, ALEXANDER, born 1816, formerly innkeeper of the Burnett Arms in Upper Banchory, Aberdeenshire, died in Upper Canada in 1846. [W.VII.688]

SIMPSON, ALEXANDER, son of Reverend Alexander Simpson in Strichen, Aberdeenshire, graduated MA from Marishcal College in 1841, later a Lieutenant Colonel of the Bengal Artillery. [MCA]

SIMPSON, CHARLES, in Fraserburgh, Aberdeenshire, a victim of rioting in 1813. [NRS.AD4.13.88]

SIMPSON, DAVID, son of Henry Simpson in Chapel of Garioch, a student at Marischal College in 1840s, later a judge in the Punjab, India. [MCA]

SIMSON, Reverend HENRY, at the Chapel of Garioch, Aberdeenshire, died 30 January 1850, father of David Simson of the Bengal Civil Service. [NRS.S/H]

SIMPSON, JAMES, of Tobago, was admitted as a burgess of Banff in 1773. [BBR]

SIMPSON, JAMES, a teacher of writing in Banff in 1809. [AOB.ii.206]

SIMPSON, JOHN, born 1738, died 20 March 1808, husband of Jane Grant, born 1743, died 27 March 1812, parents of James Simpson a merchant in Banff. [Banff gravestone]

SIMPSON, JOHN, from Banff, graduated MA from King's College, Aberdeen, on 26 March 1796. [KCA]

SIMPSON, JOHN, born 1799, son of Alexander Simpson born 1766, a shipmaster who died in London on 19 May 1810, and his wife Jean Smith, born 1766, died 8 January 1839, died in Canton, China, on 10 November 1822. [Banff gravestone]

SIMPSON, ROBERT, from Rothes, Moray, settled in Florida, Montgomery County, New York, a deed, 1812. [NRS.RD5.59.545]

SIMPSON, WILLIAM LAURENCE, son of Robert Simpson minister of the Free Church in Kintore, Aberdeenshire, at Marischal College in 1850s, later in Dunedin, Otago, New Zealand. [MCA]

SIMS, ANDREW, sometime in Jamaica, died in Peterhead, Aberdeenshire, on 9 February 1803. [Peterhead gravestone]

SIM, ANDREW, born in Ellon, Aberdeenshire, died at the plantation Garden of Eden, Demerara, on 7 August 1821. [BM.10.609]

SINGER, JAMES, born 1807, farmer at Little Folla, died 10 March 1842, husband of Isabella Gall, born 1809, died 10 August 1854. [Daviot gravestone]

SKEAF, MARY, wife of Andrew Gordon a saddler in Ballater, Aberdeenshire, later in Canada, heir to her grandfather a quill manufacturer in Edinburgh who died on 4 March 1833. [NRS.S/H]

SKELTON, JAMES, a shipmaster in Peterhead, Aberdeenshire, a sasine, 1798. [NRS.RS.Aberdeen.1755]

SKENE, ADAM, at the Mill of Glanderston, testament, 1790. Comm. Aberdeen. [NRS]

SKENE, ANDREW, minister at Banff, testament, 1793, Comm. Aberdeen. [NRS]

SKENE, CHARLOTTE, born 1847, eldest daughter of William Skene in Banchory-Tiernan, Kincardineshire, and wife of J. C. Rawlins, died in Pleasant Valley, Jefferson Davies County, Illinois, on 14 February 1876. [AJ.6689]

SKENE, ELIZA, eldest daughter of James Skene of Rubislaw, Aberdeenshire, married the Chevalier de Heidenstar, Swedish Minister to the Greek Court, in Athens, Greece, on 5 March 1840. [EEC.20041]

SKENE, HELEN, daughter of George Skene of Rubislaw, Aberdeenshire, died in Florence, Italy, on 20 July 1842. [AJ.4937] [SG.1109]

SKENE, ISOBEL, relict of John Nicolson in Auchterless, Aberdeenshire, testament, 1792, Comm. Aberdeen. [NRS]

SKENE, THOMAS, sometime in Scotstoun, afterwards at Bridge of Don, testament, 1799, Comm. Aberdeen. [NRS]

SKINNER, JOHN, Episcopal minister of Lunshart, Aberdeenshire, from 1842 until 1807. [NRS.CH12.12.2333]

SLATER, ALEXANDER, master of the Active of Peterhead, Aberdeenshire, trading between St Petersburg, Russia, and Inverness in 1806. [NRS.E504.17.8]

SLORACH, ADAM, from Fochabers, Moray, a truckman in Halifax, Nova Scotia, probate 1804, Halifax, N.S.

SMITH, ALEXANDER, in Woodend, testament, 1800, Comm. Aberdeen. [NRS]

SMITH, ALEXANDER, a writer in Edinburgh, son of Robert Smith a writer in Elgin, Moray, was admitted as a Notary Public on 8 March 1794. [NRS.NP2.35.147]

SMITH, ALEXANDER, in New York, son of James Smith in Auldearn, Nairnshire, in 1799, admin. PCC. [TNA]

SMITH, ALEXANDER, a shoemaker and militiaman, was admitted as a burgess of Elgin in 1797. [EBR]

SMITH, ALEXANDER, from Kintore, Aberdeenshire, died in New York on 19 April 1852. [AJ.12.5.1852]

SMITH, ANDREW, born 1762 in Banff, emigrated to America in 1775, a farmer in Greenville, South Carolina, in 1812, in St George's. Dorchester, by 1814, naturalised in S.C. [NARA.M1183.1]

SMITH, GEORGE, born 22 December 1808, son of James Scott, a farmer, and his wife Jean Hutcheon in Old Deer, Aberdeenshire, was educated at King's College, Aberdeen, from 1823 to 1824, a farmer in Turriff, Aberdeenshire, later a land speculator in Chicago, Illinois, in 1833, a banker in Chicago in 1839, and President of the Chicago, Milwaukee and St Paul Railroad. [KCA] [ENES.1.253] [MCA]

SMITH, H. G. L., teacher at the Madras School, a teacher of English in Banff from 1842 to 1844. [AOB.ii.207]

SMITH, JAMES, from Banff, graduated MA from King's College, Aberdeen, on 30 March 1790. [KCA]

SMITH, JAMES, born in Banffshire, was naturalised in Charleston, South Carolina, on 21 January 1799. [NARA.M1183.1]

SMITH, JAMES, born 24 August 1816, son of Alexander Smith, a shoemaker in Old Machar, and his wife Isabella Main, [1779-1827], settled in Buffalo, New York, before 1827. [Banchory Ternan gravestone, Kincardineshire]

SMITH, JAMES, parish clerk of Banff in 1834. [AOB.ii.116]

SMITH, JAMES, son of David Smith a farmer in Aboyne, Aberdeenshire, a student at Marischal College in 1830s, later a banker in Canada. [MCA]

SMITH, JAMES LAMOND, from Glen Millan, Aberdeenshire, married Isabella Barker from Warwickshire, in Guelph, Canada, on 22 October 1844. [GM.NS23.196]

SMITH, JAMES, in Sackville, New Brunswick, brother and heir of Alexander Smith a staff surgeon in MacDuff, Banffshire, who died 21 July 1848. [NRS.S/H]

SMITH, JOHN, late from Antigua, residing at Cherryvale near Aberdeen, testament, 1795, Comm. Aberdeen. [NRS]

SMITH, JOHN, a weaver in Gilmomston, testament, 1796, Comm. Aberdeen. [NRS]

SMITH, JOHN, born in Forres, Moray, a merchant in New York from 1791 until 1818. [ANY]

SMITH, JOHN, born 20 February 1811 at Cowperhill, Darnaway, Forres, Moray, died in Fayetteville, Cumberland County, North Carolina, on 17 September 1859. [Cross Creek gravestone, N.C.]

SMITH, JOHN FLEMING, in Brandywine, North America, cousin and heir of Gavin Smith in Concraig, Aberdeenshire, who died 4 January 1843. [NRS.S/H]

SMITH, JOHN, son of John Smith a blacksmith in Peterculter, Aberdeenshire, was educated at Marischal College around 1844, later Professor of Chemistry in Sydney, New South Wales, Australia. [MCA]

SMITH, LEWIS LUDOVICK, from Forres, Moray, settled in Antigua and later in St Kitts by 1821. [NRS.CS17.1.40/252]

SMITH, MARGARET, born 1817, daughter of John Smith a writer in Huntly, Aberdeenshire, wife of Alexander Gordon, died in Madoc, Upper Canada, on 21 October 1848. [AJ.5264]

SMITH, PETER, born 1792, a coppersmith from Aberdeen, died at 16 Beaver Street, Albany, New York, on 16 February 1858. [AJ.17.3.1858]

SMITH, WILLIAM, born 1750 in Longside, Aberdeenshire, a merchant in Charleston, South Carolina, from 1784 until his death on 9 April 1814. [St Michael's gravestone, Charleston]

SMITH, WILLIAM, born 1795 in Banffshire, died in Halifax, Nova Scotia, on 7 January 1819. [AR.9.1.1819]

SMITH, WILLIAM, was born in Stonehaven, Kincardineshire, a weaver in Forfar, Angus, was accused of theft in Letham, Angus, in 1822. [NRS.AD14.22.56]

SMITH, WILLIAM, son of Alexander Smith of Glenmillan an advocate in Aberdeen, a student at Marischal College around 1850, later with the Standard Insurance Company in Montreal, Quebec. [MCA]

SMITH, WILLIAM, in St Vincent, heir of James Steinson a schoolmaster in King Edward, Aberdeenshire, 1856. [NRS.S/H]

SMITH, WILLIAM, son of James Smith in Bishopmill, Moray, settled in Whitehall, St Thomas in the East, Jamaica, died there on 17 October 1865. [GM.NS3/1.143]

SMITH, ..., master of the Providence of Findhorn, Moray, trading between Wick and Aberdeen in 1790. [AJ.2225]

SONTAG, JOHN, in Danzig, was admitted as a burgess of Banff in 1800. [BBR]

SOUTAR, ALEXANDER, born 1840, second son of John Soutar a farmer in Crampstone, Kildrummy, Aberdeenshire, died aboard the Sebastapol when on passage to New Zealand in 1862. [AJ.5967]

SOUTER, FRANCIS, agent for the Commercial Bank of Scotland in Turriff, Aberdeenshire, in 1849. [POD]

SOUTAR, JAMES WILLIAM, born 1823, youngest son of William Soutar a farmer in Auchlin, died at his brother's house in Sandusky, Ohio, on 14 May 1849. [AJ.5293]

SOUTAR, JOHN, a skipper in Peterhead, inventory, 1807, Comm. Aberdeen. [NRS]

SOUTAR, STEWART, born 1834, son of Alexander Soutar a writer in Banff, died in Malmesbury, Cape of Good Hope, South Africa, on 18 November 1861. [AJ.5947][EEC.23674]

SOUTAR, WILLIAM, a shipmaster in Peterhead, son of John Soutar a shipmaster in Peterhead, a sasine, 1796. [NRS.RS.Aberdeen.1609]

SPALDING, PETER, a farm servant at Culter, Aberdeenshire, testament, 1795, Comm. Aberdeen. [NRS]

SPARK, ALEXANDER, born 7 January 1762 in Marykirk, Kincardineshire, son of John Spark and his wife Mary Low, was educated at King's College, Aberdeen, emigrated to Quebec in 1780, a teacher and a minister, married Mary Ross in Quebec on 13 July 1805, died there on 7 March 1819. [DCB][KCA]

SPENCE, ALEXANDER, from Banff, graduated MA from King's College, Aberdeen, on 27 March 1795. [KCA]

SPENCE, JAMES, born 1762 in Banffshire, settled in New Brunswick in 1783, died in Hampton, N.B., on 29 March 1828. [NBC.5.4.1828]

STALKER, JOHN, from Aberlour, Banffshire, graduated MA in 1858 from King's College, Aberdeen, a missionary in Pietermaritzburg, Natal, South Africa. [KCA]

STEEL, WILLIAM, born 1842, son of William Steel a slater in Banff, died at Key West Hospital, in the Bahamas, on 7 October 1865. [AJ.22.3.1865]

STEINSON, JAMES, from Fordyce, Banffshire, graduated MA from King's College, Aberdeen, in March 1834, later a teacher in England. [KCA]

STEPHEN, ALEXANDER, in Farmtoun of Balfluig, testament, 1800, Comm. Aberdeen. [NRS]

STEPHEN, ALEXANDER, son of John Stephen, a baker in Rothes, Moray, [died in 1854], and his wife Anne Booth, [died 1841], settled in America before 1877. [Rothes gravestone]

STEPHEN, ALEXANDER, the younger, a seaman on a Greenland ship, residing in Old Middleton, Aberdeenshire, was accused of mobbing and rioting in 1813. [NRS.AD4.13.88]

STEPHEN, JOHN, born 1840, son of James Stephen and his wife Jane Craig, died in Alameda, California, on 13 July 1892. [Dunnottar gravestone, Kincardineshire]

STEPHEN, JOSEPH, born 1 January 1797 in Fordoun, Kincardineshire, son of Alexander Stephen farmer of the Mains of Glenfarquhar, and his wife Isobel Robertson, died in Jamaica on 15 January 1821. [Fordoun gravestone][S.224.143]

STEPHEN, RACHEL, spouse to James Deans a merchant in Old Meldrum, Aberdeenshire, testament, 1794, Comm. Aberdeen. [NRS]

STEPHEN, ROBERT, jr., born 1810, late a farmer in Balbride, Durris, Kincardineshire, died in Knoxville, Knox County, Illinois, on 4 March 1844. [AJ.6024]

STEPHEN, ROBERT, agent in Fraserburgh, Aberdeenshire, for the North of Scotland Bank in 1849. [POD]

STEPHEN, ROBERT, born 23 August 1851, died in South Africa, on 23 May 1897. [St George gravestone, Port Elizabeth, Cape of Good Hope]

STEPHEN, WILLIAM, born 25 March 1801 in Dufftown, Banffshire, son of William Stephen of Hillside and his wife Elizabeth Cameron, married Elspet Smith from Knockando, Moray, in 1828, settled in Montreal, Quebec. [BCG]

STEPHEN, WILLIAM, in West Cults, Aberdeenshire, father of William Stephen born 1852, died in San Diego, Texas, on 26 October 1878. [AJ.4.11.1878]

STEVENSON, JAMES, born 1777 in Aberdeenshire, died in Annapolis, Nova Scotia, in April 1826. [AR.8.4.1826]

STEPHENSON, JOHN, master of the Kitty of Portsoy, Banffshire, trading between Easdale and Inverness in 1805. [NRS.E504.17.8]

STEVENSON, WILLIAM, a foxhunter in Stonehaven, Kincardineshire, a decreet, 1811. [NRS.GD45.18.2351]

STEUART, GEORGE, a Writer to the Signet, eldest son of Patrick Steuart of Tannachy, Banffshire, was admitted as a Notary Public on 2 June 1792, died 25 October 1814. [NRS.NP2.34.343]

STEWART, ALEXANDER, son of Reverend Patrick Stewart in Kinneff, Kincardineshire, a student at Marischal College around 1820, later an assistant surgeon in the Service of the East India Company. [MCA]

STEWART, ALEXANDER, married Eliza Stephen, both from Moray, in Halifax, Nova Scotia, in 1833. [AR.11.5.1833]

STEWART, ALEXANDER, born in Banffshire, died at Musquodoboit, Nova Scotia, on 2 May 1841. [AR.22.5.1841]

STEWART, ANDREW, youngest son of Patrick Stewart of Tannochie, Aberdeenshire, died in Jamaica in September 1794. [SM.56.801]

STEWART, Mrs ANN, born 1755 in Banffshire, died in Halifax, Nova Scotia, on 4 July 1834. [AR.5.7.1834]

STEWART, CHARLES, from Forres, Moray, graduated MA from King's College, Aberdeen, on 23 January 1847, later a merchant in America. [KCA]

STEWART, JAMES, in Elnoch, Glen Muick, Aberdeenshire, a prisoner in Aberdeen Tolbooth, was sentenced to be transported beyond the seas, on 7 April 1796. [NRS.JC11.42]

STEWART, JAMES, from Banff, graduated MA from King's College, Aberdeen, on 29 March 1799. [KCA]

STEWART, JAMES, a Captain of the 3rd Battalion of the Royal Scots Regiment, son of Andrew Stewart of Auchlunkart, Banffshire, died at St Sebastian, Spain, on 2 September 1799. [SM.75.799]

STEWART, JAMES, in Huntly, Aberdeenshire, brother and heir of John Stewart in the West Indies, 1854. [NRS.S/H]

STEWART, JOHN, 'an Excise delinquent', escaped from Banff jail in 1825. [Annals of Banff.i.354]

STEWART, PATRICK, son of Reverend Patrick Stewart in Kinneff, Kincardineshire, a student at Marischal College from 1812 to 1815, later with the Customs House in London. [MCA]

STEWART, PETER, a contractor in Canada, son and heir of Peter Stewart, an innkeeper in Strichen, Aberdeenshire, 1839. [NRS.S/H]

STEWART, ROBERT, from Banffshire, a merchant in Petersburg, Virginia, testament, 1816, Comm. Edinburgh. [NRS]

STEWART, THOMAS JOHN, a surgeon in Kincardine O'Neil, Aberdeenshire, testament, 1797, Comm. Aberdeen. [NRS]

STEWART, WILLIAM, son of James Stewart a farmer in Hazlehead, Aberdeenshire, in Jamaica, a sasine, 1796. [NRS.RS54.PR38/27]

STEWART, WILLIAM, agent for the Bank of Scotland in Stonehaven, Kincardineshire, in 1849. [POD]

STEWART, ..., master of the Nelly and Peggy of Fraserburgh, captured by a French privateer off Norway in 1798. [AJ.2637]

STILLAS, ALEXANDER, a merchant in Old Meldrum, Aberdeenshire, testament, 1790, Comm. Aberdeen. [NRS]

STRACHAN, Mrs HELEN, born 1824, wife of James Strachan, from Fortree of Esslemont, Ellon, Aberdeenshire, died in Rochester, New York, on 8 April 1874. [AJ.6.5.1874]

STRACHAN, JAMES, from Banff, graduated MA from King's College, Aberdeen, on 29 March 1793. [KCA]

STRACHAN, JAMES, the elder, at the Mains of Arnage, Ellon, Aberdeenshire, a victim of theft in 1836. [NRS.AD14.36.170]

STRACHAN, JOHN, born 1763, from Campfield, Kincardine O'Neil, Aberdeenshire, emigrated to America in 1819, died in Waterford, New York, in 1850. [AJ.5340]

STRACHAN, WILLIAM, a merchant in Peterhead, Aberdeenshire, father of Frederick Strachan who died in Keysville, Harboro, Florida, on 1 July 1884. [S.12808]

STRACHAN, ..., master of the Hope of Portsoy, Banffshire, trading between Leith and Scallawayvoe in 1798. [AJ.2644]

STRATH, JOHN, born in 1839, son of William Strath in the Glack of Botriphnie, Banffshire, died in Chicago, Illinois, on 25 May 1870. [AJ.15.6.1870]

STRONACH, GEORGE, a mariner in Garmouth, testament, 1826, Comm. Moray. [NRS]

STRONACH, JOHN, master of the Britannia of Nairn trading between Inverness and Limerick in 1812. [NRS.E504.17.8]

STUART, ADAM, born 1836, son of John Stuart and his wife Anne Rae, died off Cape Horn on 13 February 1869. [Strachan gravestone, Kincardineshire]

STUART, ALEXANDER, from Inveraven, Banffshire, graduated MA from King's College, Aberdeen, in March 1843, later a Congregational minister in Halifax, Nova Scotia. [KCA]

STUART, CHARLES, born 27 September 1841 in Banchory, Aberdeenshire, died in Port Elizabeth, Cape of Good Hope, South Africa, on 2 April 1875. [St George gravestone, Port Elizabeth]

STUART, JOHN P., son of Alexander Stuart of Leslie House, Leslie, Aberdeenshire, was apprenticed to Alexander Mitchell a merchant in Aberdeen in 1791. [ACA]

STUART, JOHN, in Nickerie, Surinam, eldest son of William Stewart at the Kirk of Forgue, Aberdeenshire, died in Trinidad on 19 September 1807. [SM.70.78]

STUART, ROBERT, born 1770, second son of John Stuart in Birkenburn, Banff, settled in Port Morant, Jamaica, died in Hampshire on 29 June 1813. [GM.83.666]

STUART, WALTER LAWSON, son of Alexander Stuart of Laithers an advocate, was at Marischal College in 1850s, later in Foochoo, China. [MCA]

STUART, WILLIAM, born 1823, grandson of John Stuart a farmer in Old Castle of Balvenie, Mortlach, Banffshire, died in Belrch, Mavidere, Warren County, New York, in 1849. [AJ.25.4.1849]

SUMMERS, GEORGE, a sailor on the Nancy of Stonehaven, Kincardineshire, was accused of assault and battery in 1821. [NRS.AD14.21.130]

SUTER, ALEXANDER, master of the <u>Daphne of Peterhead,</u> Aberdeenshire, trading between Fort William and Inverness in 1807. [NRS.E504.17.8]

SUTHERLAND, Mrs ELIZA, daughter of William Robertson of Cuttlebrae, Enzie, Banffshire, and daughter in law of William Sutherland in Cullen, Banffshire, died in New York on 16 January 1861. [AJ.13.2.1861]

SUTHERLAND, GEORGE, one of the sergeants of Banff, was dismissed from service on 16 March 1829. [Annals of Banff.i.354]

SUTHERLAND, JAMES, born 1773 in Elgin, Moray, a merchant who was naturalised in Charleston, South Carolina, on 21 March 1803. [NARA.M1183.1]

SUTHERLAND, JAMES, a plasterer in Boston, Massachusetts, nephew and heir of Margaret Watt a feuar in Fochabers, Moray, who died 14 July 1867. [NRS.S/H]

SUTHERLAND, JOHN, born 1818, son of William Sutherland a fishery officer in Cullen, Banffshire, a merchant who died in New York on 25 July 1861. [AJ.14.8.1861]

SUTHERLAND, JOHN, from Duffus, Moray, graduated MA from King's College, Aberdeen, in March 1842, later a planter in South Africa. [KCA]

SUTTER, Mrs ELIZABETH, born 1805 in Aberdeenshire, died in South Africa on 9 May 1866. [St George gravestone, Port Elizabeth, Cape of Good Hope.]

SUTTER, GEORGE SKELTON, born 5 June 1821 in Peterhead, Aberdeenshire, died in South Africa on 23 May 1903. [St George gravestone, Port Elizabeth, Cape of Good Hope.]

SYME, or SIM, ALEXANDER, in Auchines, Rathen, Aberdeenshire, testament, 1792, Comm. Aberdeen. [NRS]

SYME, or SIM, GEORGE, in Overhill, Tarves, Aberdeenshire, testament, 1794, Comm. Aberdeen. [NRS]

TAIT, THOMAS, a farmer in Crichie, Aberdeenshire, nephew and heir of John Tait formerly a cooper in Jamaica, later in Aberdeen, 1858. [NRS.S/H]

TAIT, WILLIAM, third son of Charles Tait and his wife Mary Erskine in Craigmill, Chapel of Garioch, Aberdeenshire, died at Annetto Bay, St George's, Jamaica, on 5 June 1826. [SAA][BM.21.119]

TARRAS, JOHN JACOB, son of Laurence Tarras, a merchant in Gothenburg, Sweden, was admitted as a burgess of Banff in 1802. [BBR]

TAWSE, JOHN, son of James Tawse, a farmer in Towie, Aberdeenshire, was educated at King's College, Aberdeen, from 1817 to 1821, later a minister in Toronto. [KCA]

TAWSE, WILIAM, son of William Tawse, [1767-1858], and his wife Elizabeth McKenzie, [1779-1848], settled in Guelph, Canada. [Birse gravestone, Aberdeenshire]

TAYLOR, BARBARA, wife of Alexander Taylor a fisher in Fraserburgh, Aberdeenshire, was accused of mobbing and rioting there in 1813. [NRS.AD4.13.88]

TAYLOR, GEORGE, son of John Taylor in Turreff, Aberdeenshire, a student in Marischal College in 1790s. [MCA]

TAYLOR, GEORGE, an elder of the parish of Banff in 1834. [AOB.ii.116]

TAYLOR, GEORGE, born 1802, late of the Mill of Inchmarlo, Upper Banchory, Aberdeenshire, died in Detroit, Michigan, on 19 July 1849. [AJ.5303]

TAYLOR, ISAAC, born 1762 in Marykirk, Kincardineshire, died in New Bern, North Carolina, on 4 July 1846. [Cedar Grove gravestone, Craven County, N.C.]

TAYLOR, JAMES, born 17 June 1798, son of William Taylor, a farmer in Coullie, Fordoun, Kincardineshire, and his wife Helen Walker, later a merchant in Savanna, Georgia. [Fordoun gravestone]

TAYLOR, JAMES, from Fochabers, Moray, applied to settle in Canada in 1815. [NRS.RH9]

TAYLOR, JOHN, from Banff, graduated MA from King's College, Aberdeen, on 28 March 1794. [KCA]

TAYLOR, JOHN, from Banff, graduated MA from King's College, Aberdeen, in March 1829, later an Episcopal minister in Cuminestone. [KCA]; born 1808, died in Huntly, Aberdeenshire, in 1857. [Ruthven gravestone, Aberdeenshire]

TAYLOR, JOHN FALCONER, a messenger at arms in Turriff, Aberdeenshire, was accused of forgery and fraud in 1838. [NRS.AD14.38.60]

TAYLOR, JOHN, born 1841, brother of W. L. Taylor a bookseller in Peterhead, Aberdeenshire, died in Nashville, Tennessee, on 24 November 1863 of wounds received at the Battle of Chickamanga on 20 September 1863, in which he served as a Sergeant of the 96th Illinois Volunteers. [S.2660][AJ.30.12.1863]

TAYLOR, WILLIAM, a merchant in Peterhead, Aberdeenshire, testament, 1795, Comm. Aberdeen. [NRS]

TAYLOR, WILLIAM, minister at New Deer, Aberdeenshire, testament, 1800, Comm. Aberdeen. [NRS]

TAYLOR, WILLIAM, master of the Mary of Peterhead, Aberdeenshire, trading between Ballachulish and Inverness in 1813. [NRS.E504.17.8]

TAYLOR, WILLIAM, a seaman from Moray, died aboard the brigantine Dove when bound from Berbice to Halifax, Nova Scotia, on 19 June 1831. [AR.2.7.1831]

TAYLOR, WILLIAM, a farmer from Thomastown, Drumblade, Aberdeenshire, died on passage from New Orleans, Louisiana, to St Louis, Missouri, on 30 March 1842. [AJ.8.6.1842]

TAYLOR, W. L., agent of the Aberdeen Bank in Cullen in 1849. [POD]

TEMPLE, JAMES, born 1822, fourth son of Robert Temple in Cloisterseat, Udny, Aberdeenshire, died in Port Dover. Upper Canada, on 26 December 1845. [AJ.5120]

TESTARD, JAMES, in Luidmuic of Glen Muick, testament, 1800, Comm. Aberdeen. [NRS]

THAIN, JOHN, son of John Thain of Drumblair, Forgue, Aberdeenshire, a student at Marischal College in 1830s, later a sheep farmer in Queensland, Australia. [MCA]

THAIN, MARY, in Fraserburgh, Aberdeenshire, was accused of mobbing and rioting there in 1813. [NRS.AD4.13.88]

THAIN, THOMAS, born 1779, son of John Thain, 1739-1816, settled in Montreal, Quebec, died 1832. [Forgue gravestone, Aberdeenshire]

THIRD, ELSPET, from Aberdeenshire, widow of Lewis Burnett, died in Lockport, Illinois, on 13 April 1858. [AJ.16.6.1858]

THOM, ALEXANDER, son of William Thom at Berryhillock, Aberdeenshire, a writer in Aberdeen, was admitted as a Notary Public on 30 June 1791. [NRS. NP2.34.271]

THOM. JOHN, born 1825, son of William Thom and his wife Mary Burnett, died in Coraki, New South Wales, Australia, on 2 September 1869. [Banchory Ternan gravestone, Aberdeenshire]

THOM, WILLIAM, a farmer in Glascoforest, Kinellar, Aberdeenshire, father of William Thom who died in St Charles, Illinois, on 25 January 1852. [AJ.10.3.1852]

THOMSON, ELSPET, in Kingswells, relict of Alexander Ramsay a vintner in Old Meldrum, Aberdeenshire, testament, 1797, Comm. Aberdeen. [NRS]

THOMSON, GEORGE, from Banff, graduated MA from King's College, Aberdeen, on 29 March 1792, later minister at Fetteresso, Kincardineshire. [KCA]

THOMSON, GEORGE, a ship's carpenter from Kincardineshire, was naturalised in Charleston, South Carolina, on 15 January 1828. [NARA.M1183.1]

THOMSON, GEORGE, born 1824 in Ellon, Aberdeenshire, emigrated in 1843, died in Fairfield, Tobago, on 24 November 1846. [AJ.5169]

THOMSON, H. R., agent in Garmouth, Moray, for the Caledonian Bank in 1849. [POD]

THOMSON, JAMES, from Banff, graduated MA from King's College, Aberdeen, on 27 March 1800. [KCA]

THOMSON, JAMES, born 1781, farmer in Knowhead, Marnoch, died 21 January 1856, husband of Elizabeth Bremner, born 1783, died 19 June 1868. [Rathven gravestone, Aberdeenshire]

THOMSON, Mrs JANET, born 1751 in Banffshire, died in Halifax, Nova Scotia, on 23 October 1835. [AR.24.10.1835]

THOMSON, JAMES, born 1819, son of Alexander Thomson a feuar in Fochabers, Moray, and his wife Elspet Geddes, died in Adelaide, South Australia, on 10 April 1878. [Speymouth Dipple gravestone, Moray]

THOMSON, JOHN, in Howboat, testament, 1800, Comm. Aberdeen. [NRS]

THOMSON, JOHN, born 1793, son of John Thomson, a shoemaker in Aberdeen, and his wife Margaret Mitchell, died in Jamaica in December 1830. [Banchory Devenick gravestone]

THOMSON, JOHN, born 1806, second son of John Thomson a merchant in Stonehaven, Kincardineshire, a millwright who died in Launceston, Van Diemen's Land, [Tasmania], Australia, on 19 February 1838. [AJ.4723]

THOMSON, JOHN, born 1807, son of James Thomson in Stonehaven, Stonehaven, a Captain of the 5th Regiment of the Madras Native Infantry, died in Trichinopoly, India, on 19 September 1839. [AJ.5496]

THOMSON, MARGARET, only daughter of Andrew Thomson of Banchory, Aberdeenshire, testament, 1800, Comm. Aberdeen. [NRS]

THOMSON, ROBERT, from Rothes, Moray, graduated MA from King's College, Aberdeen, in March 1833, later minister at Peterculter. [KCA]

THOMSON, WILLIAM, born 1762 in Elgin, Moray, settled in Nova Scotia in 1806, died in Antigonish, N.S., on 5 July 1830. [HJ.12.7.1830]

THOMSON, WILLIAM, born 1786, son of John Thomson a feuar in Dufftown, Banffshire, and his wife Jane Grant, died in Jamaica in 1811. [Aberlour gravestone, Banffshire]

THOMSON, WILLIAM, a slater and shipowner in Stonehaven, Kincardineshire, died 28 January 1849, father of James Thomson who settled in Jacksonville, Oregon, before 1888. [NRS.S/H.1888]

THOMSON, WILLIAM, a surgeon in Stonehaven, Kincardineshire, died on 21 April 1858, father of William Gordon Thomson in Elkadua, Ceylon. [NRS.S/H.1867]

THORBURN, ALEXANDER, agent in Keith, Banffshire, for the Aberdeen Town and County Bank in 1849. [POD]

THURBURN, ALEXANDER, son of Alexander Thurburn of Drumduan, a student at Marischal College in 1850s, latera merchant in Shanghai, China. [MCA]

TOCHER, WILLIAM, [1841-1909], and his wife Margaret Barclay, [1844-1920], parents of John Tocher, born 1871, died in California in 1888. [Tyrie gravestone, Aberdeenshire]

TOD, or TODDIE, ANDREW, in London, heir to Lindsay Tod or Toddie a cotton planter in America, 1833. [NRS.S/H]

TOD, or TODDIE, or MCGREGOR, BETTY, in London, heir to Lindsay Tod or Toddie a cotton planter in America, 1833. [NRS.S/H]

TOD, or TODDIE, or MURDOCH, ELSPETH, in Dyce, Aberdeenshire, heir to Lindsay Tod or Toddie a cotton planter in America, 1833. [NRS.S/H]

TODD, JOSEPH, from the Mearns, Kincardineshire, graduated MA from King's College, Aberdeen, on 27 March 1795. [KCA]

TOPP, ALEXANDER, from Moray, graduated MA from King's College, Aberdeen, in March 1831, later a minister of the Free Church in Toronto, Canada. [KCA]

TOPP, JAMES, born 1781, died in Jamaica in 1835. [Daviot gravestone]

TOPP, WILLIAM, son of Alexander Topp a farmer in Elgin, Moray, graduated MA from Marischal College in 1826, later a merchant on the Gold Coast, West Africa, and a farmer at Inverlochty, Elgin, Moray. [MCA]

TORRIE, JOHN, son of Bishop John Torrie in Peterhead, Aberdeenshire, graduated MA from Marischal College in 1818, later a minister in Coupar Angus. [MCA]

TOUGH, JAMES, in the Mains of Drum, Drumoak, Aberdeenshire, father of James Tough who died in St Louis, Missouri, on 18 June 1872. [AJ.10.7.1872]

TROUP, WILLIAM, a minister in Hamilton, Canada West, son and heir of William Troup in Dalbhadie, Aberdeenshire, who died on 1 March 1858. [NRS.S/H]

TURING, Reverend Sir INGLIS, of Foveran, Aberdeenshire, Rector of St Thomas in the Vale, Jamaica, died there in November 1791. [GM.61.1235][EEC.11488]

TURNBULL, WILLIAM, formerly a farmer in Lochend of Barra, Aberdeenshire, later in San Francisco, California, died in New York on 18 November 1869. [AJ.15.12.1869]

TURNBULL, Mrs, from Fochabers, Moray, died in Demerara on 1 February 1801. [GC.1519]

TURNER, JOHN, son of John Turner of Turnerhall and his wife Elizabeth Urquhart, died in Grenada on 2 June 1792. [AJ]

TURNER, ROBERT, the sheriff substitute of Aberdeenshire, testament, 1794, Comm. Aberdeen. [NRS]

TURNER, ROBERT, in Keith, Banffshire, graduated MD from King's College, Aberdeen, on 31 July 1843. [KCA]

TURNER, THOMAS ANDREW, son of Robert Turner the Sheriff Substitute of Aberdeenshire, was apprenticed to Thomas Bannerman a merchant in Aberdeen in 1791. [ACA]; a merchant in Montreal, Quebec, appointed Maxwell Gordon a Writer to the Signet as his attorney re the estate of Turnerhall, in 1804. [NRS.RD3.304/1.245]

TURNER, WILLIAM DONALDSON, born 26 February 1784, son of Robert Thomson of Menie, Belhelvie, Aberdeenshire, and his wife Euphemia Simpson, a soldier from 1800 until his death at Mirzapur, India, on 24 June 1813, a Captain Lieutenant of the 15th Native Infantry of the Bengal Army. [BA.4.329]

URE, DUNCAN, a teacher in Kincardine, died in November 1831, brother of David Ure in Dunedin, New Zealand. [NRS.S/H.1866]

URQUHART, Captain JOHN, son of William Urquhart of Craigstoun, was appointed as a trustee of Dr John Anderson of St Kitts in 1796. [NRS.RD2.278.744]

URQUHART, JOHN, of Craigstoun, was admitted as a burgess of Banff in 1800. [BBR]

URQUHART, R., agent in Forres, Moray, for the Caledonian Banking Company in 1849. [POD]

VOLUM, WILLIAM, a shipmaster in Peterhead, Aberdeenshire, son of James Volum a surgeon in Peterhead, a sasine, 1798. [NRS.RS.Aberdeen.1822]

WALKER, ALEXANDER, son of James Walker in Lumphanan, Aberdeenshire, a student in Marischal College in 1790s. [MCA]

WALKER, ANDREW, [1819-1901], a farmer in Torphins, Aberdeenshire, and his wife Susan Gerrard, [1819-1897], parents of William G. Walker who settled in Ookala, Hawaii. [Banchory Devenick gravestone, Kincardineshire]

WALKER, JOHN, born in Aberdeenshire, settled in St Croix, Danish West Indies, died in Glasgow on 11 July 1809. [SM.71.560]

WALKER, ROBERT DUFF, born 15 March 1846, son of Reverend John Walker and his wife Anne Duff in St Andrew's parish, Moray, settled in Australia, died there on 29 December 1898.

WALKER, W.P., son of David Walker a farmer in Upper Park, Aberdeenshire, died in Grenada on 27 October 1838. [AJ.30.1.1839]

WALLACE, ALEXANDER, in Shore Street, Fraserburgh, Aberdeenshire, was accused of theft, trial papers, 1831. [NRS.JC26.1831.58]

WALLACE, ALEXANDER, a farmer at Mormond, Aberdeenshire, grandfather of Alexander Wallace, a merchant in Calcutta, India. [NRS.S/H.1847]

WALLACE, ISAAC, in Nairnshire, graduated MD from King's College, Aberdeen, on 26 July 1847. [KCA]

WALLIS, JAMES, born 1823, son of William Wallis in Gartly, was educated at Marischal College in 1840s, later minister in Woodside, Aberdeenshire, from 1849 to 1854, a minister in Demerara from 1854, a minister in New Zealand from 1865. [F.6.42][MCA]

WARDLAW, WILLIAM, of Whitehill, died in Damascus on 15 June 1837. [AJ.4675]

WARRACK, CHARLES, born 1797, son of John Warrack in the New Mill of Fintry, Aberdeenshire, died at Mount Grace, Tobago, on 1 October 1822. [SM.91.127]

WATSON, JAMES, master of the Industry of Portsoy, Banffshire, trading between Fort William and Inverness in 1807. [NRS.E504.17.8]; inventory, 1821, Comm. Aberdeen. [NRS]

WATSON, JAMES, master of the Diamond of Peterhead, Aberdeenshire, trading between Easdale and Inverness, 1807. [NRS.E504.17.8]

WATSON, JOHN FORBES, from Strathdon, Aberdeenshire, graduated MA in March 1847, also MD from King's College, Aberdeen, on 5 August 1848, later in the Service of the East India Company. [KCA]

WATSON, ROBERT, late of Stoneywood, Aberdeenshire, died in Detroit, Michigan, on 11 March 1848, his son James Watson also died there but on 24 January 1848. [AJ.5285]

WATSON, R., agent for the National Bank of Scotland in Forres, Moray, in 1849. [POD]

WATSON, WILLIAM, born 1801, feuar in New Aberdour, husband of Mary Cardno, born 1801, died 29 April 1892, parents of John Watson in Montreal, Quebec. [Aberdour gravestone, Aberdeenshire]

WATSON, Mr, a surgeon, reported a case of cholera on the Low Shore of Banff on 16 July 1833. [Annals of Banff.i.358]

WATT, Mrs AGNES GLENNIE, from Inverurie, Aberdeenshire, died in St George's Plain Estate, Savanna la Mar, Jamaica, on 8 September 1865. [AJ.4.11.1863]

WATT, ALEXANDER, from New Deer, Aberdeenshire, later in Canada, son and heir of Isabella Norrie or Watt in Auchreddie, Aberdeenshire, 1836. [NRS.S/H]

WATT, CHARLES, a shipmaster in Banff, husband of Lucinda Pirie, born 1788, died 7 March 1813. [Banff gravestone]

WATT, or TOWNSLEY, FORBES, in Yorkville, Canada West, heir to his uncle Charles Watt a solicitor in Banff who died 20 September 1845. [NRS.S/H]

WATT, GEORGE, born 1831, eldest son of George Watt in Broad Street, Fraserburgh, Aberdeenshire, died in Brooklyn, New York, on 23 June 1868. [S.7788]

WATT, JAMES, from Cairnie, Aberdeenshire, died on Montreuil Estate in Grenada on 29 August 1863. [AJ.4.11.1863]

WATT, JOHN, in India, provided money for the poor of Banff in 1802. [Annals of Banff.ii.113]

WATT, PETER, from Banff, graduated MA from King's College, Aberdeen, on 28 March 1799. [KCA]

WATT, WILLIAM, from Kincardine, graduated MA from King's College, Aberdeen, in March 1829, later a schoolmaster in Durris, Kincardineshire, and a minister in Foveran, Aberdeenshire. [KCA]

WATT, WILLIAM, from Macduff, Banffshire, father of William George Watt an infant who died in New York in 1857. [AJ.2.9.1857]

WATTIE, JAMES, a merchant in Strathdon, Aberdeenshire, father of James Wattie, born 1850, died in Parker, Kansas, on 27 August 1871. [AJ.10.4.1872]

WEBSTER, ALEXANDER, from Banff, graduated MA from King's College, Aberdeen, on 27 March 1795. [KCA]

WEBSTER, GEORGE, farmer in Collarlie, testament, 1792, Comm. Aberdeen. [NRS]

WEBSTER, JAMES, son of Alexander Webster a farmer in Mondynes, Fordoun, Kincardineshire, graduated MA from Marischal College in 1817, later a schoolmaster in Farnell and in Crail. [MCA]

WEBSTER, JAMES, born 1827, in the Mains of Inveramsie, died 18 December 1867, husband of Barbara Neil, born 1822, died 8 March 1907. [Daviot gravestone]

WEIR, FRANCIS, from Cromar, Aberdeenshire, graduated MA from King's College, Aberdeen, on 30 March 1791. [KCA]

WEIR, GEORGE, from Aberlour, Banffshire, graduated MA from King's College, Aberdeen, in March 1848, later Professor of Classics in Kingston, Quebec. [KCA]

WELSH, DAVID, [1799-1876], and his wife Jane White, [1799-1882], father of David Welsh, born 1837, died in Washington on 26 September 1883. [Fettercairn gravestone, Kincardineshire]

WERNHAM, FRANCIS, third son of William Wernham a factor in Troup, Banffshire, was murdered by natives in Moboli in the Solomon Islands on 10 May 1872. [AJ.6511]

WHITE, ALEXANDER, born 1814 in Elgin, Moray, died in Rosedale, Lake Forest, Illinois, on 18 March 1872. [NRS.S/H]

WHITE, WILLIAM, from Fraserburgh, Aberdeenshire, a shopkeeper in Charleston, South Carolina, probate 18 July 1793, Charleston, S.C.; probate January 1795, PCC. [TNA]

WHITNEY, JOHN B., born in Fochabers, Moray, around 1780, died in Charleston, South Carolina, on 13 December 1817. [Unitarian gravestone, Charleston]

WHYTE, AGNES, born 1818, daughter of Joseph Whyte a surgeon in Banff, wife of J. Whyte, died at 43 Queen Street, Charleston, South Carolina, in 1842, mother of a son born on 29 July 1842. [AJ.4940]

WHYTE, ALEXANDER, son of Alexander Whyte in Fettercairn, Kincardineshire, at Marischal College around 1850, later in Ceylon. [MCA]

WHYTE, JAMES SHAND, eldest son of Reverend Alexander Whyte in Fettercairn, Kincardineshire, died in Gouyave, Grenada, on 14 December 1859. [S.1436][DC.23470]

WHYTE, JOHN, born 1803 in Banff, a surgeon who died in Sydney, Nova Scotia, on 24 July 1828. [AR.20.9.1828]

WHYTE, JOSEPH, son of William Whyte a farmer in Pitsligo, Aberdeenshire, a student at Marischal College in 1830s, later a schoolmaster in Fraserburgh, Aberdeenshire, then in Charleston, South Carolina, and Montreal, Quebec. [MCA]

WHYTE, WILLIAM, a shipmaster in Peterhead, Aberdeenshire, husband of Christian Livingston, a sasine, 1790. [NRS.RS.Aberdeen.858]; testament, 1792, Comm. Aberdeen. [NRS]

WILLIAM, PETER, a shoemaker in Craigielae, testament, 1793, Comm. Aberdeen. [NRS]

WILLIAMSON, ALEXANDER, from Jamaica, later in the Haugh of Edinglassie, testament, 1791, Comm. Aberdeen. [NRS]

WILLIAMSON, ALEXANDER, in the Haugh of Edinglassie, testament, 1796, Comm. Aberdeen. [NRS]

WILLIAMSON, D., from Bell's Institution in Edinburgh, a teacher of English in Banff in 1847-1848. [AOB.ii.207]

WILLIAMSON, JOHN, born 1805, son of John Williamson and his wife Jane Russell, died in Jamaica on 16 November 1850. [Speymouth Dipple gravestone, Moray]

WILLIAMSON, ROBERT, born 26 July 1806, son of Robert Williamson, a farmer in the Mains of Port Lethan, and his wife Elizabeth, died in Tobago in 1827. [Banchory Devenick gravestone, Aberdeenshire]

WILSON, ADAM, son of John Wilson in Montgrew, Banffshire, died in Bossue, Manchester, Jamaica, on 10 November 1850. [AJ.5374]

WILSON, ALEXANDER, from Cullen, Banffshire, graduated MA from King's College, Aberdeen, in March 1834, later a surgeon in the Royal Navy. [KCA]

WILSON, ALEXANDER, son of John Wilson a farmer in Cullen, Banffshire, a student at Marischal College around 1850, later a merchant in Calcutta, India. [MCA]

WILSON, Dr DAVID, late of Finzeauch, a physician in Peterhead, testament, 1791, Comm. Aberdeen. [NRS]

WILSON, ELIZABETH, relict of Alexander Strachan minister at Keig, testament 1791, Comm. Aberdeen. [NRS]

WILSON, GEORGE, son of Lieutenant Peter Wilson, an accountant from Keith, Banffshire, died on the Cape Coast, South Africa, on 24 June 1839. [AJ.4788]

WILSON, GEORGE, from Insch, Aberdeenshire, a student at King's College, Aberdeen, in 1841, later a teacher in America. [KCA]

WILSON, HENRY THOMAS, from Gamrie, Banffshire, graduated MA from King's College, Aberdeen, in March 1851. [KCA]

WILSON, ISAAC, a shipmaster in Banff, inventory, 1815, Comm. Aberdeen. [NRS]

WILSON, JAMES, from Gamrie, Banffshire, graduated MA from King's College, Aberdeen, in March 1842, later a teacher in America. [KCA]

WILSON, JAMES, late in Grenada, left £8388.9 shillings, and 4 pence to the community of Banff, in 1833. [Annals of Banff.i.358]

WILSON, JAMES, born 1832, late of the *Nairnshire Telegraph* died in Shanghai, China, on 24 August 1862. [AJ.5991]

WILSON, JAMES, son of Henry Wilson a farmer in Clatt, Aberdeenshire, was educated at Marischal College in 1855, later a farmer in New Zealand. [MCA]

WILSON, JAMES, son of David Wilson an Episcopalian minister in Fyvie, Aberdeenshire, a student at Marischal College around 1850, later in Sydney, New South Wales, Australia. [MCA]

WILSON, JAMES MILNE, son of John Milne a shipowner in Banff, settled in Van Diemen's Land, Tasmania, Australia, before 1852. [NRS.S/H]

WILSON, Mrs JEANNIE, born 1846, daughter of Alexander Milne in the Mains of Esslemont, Aberdeenshire, died in St Joseph's, Trinidad, on 16 December 1874. [AJ.20.1.1875]

WILSON, JOHN, from Banff, graduated MA from King's College, Aberdeen, on 27 March 1795. [KCA]

WILSON, JOHN, a millwright in New York, son and heir of J. Wilson a farm servant in Buchan, Aberdeenshire, 1834. [NRS.S/H]

WILSON, PETER, born 1794 in Aberchirder, Banffshire, died in Duke Street, Dunedin, Otago, New Zealand, on 26 March 1876. [AJ.6699]

WILSON, ROBERT, born 1776 in Elgin, Moray, died in Halifax, Nova Scotia, on 20 August 1834. [HJ.15.9.1834]

WILSON, ROBERT, born 26 February 1791 in Cluny, son of Nathaniel Wilson, farmer at the Mill of Kincardine, and his wife Euphemia Angus, died in Jamaica on 19 December 1814. [Aboyne gravestone, Aberdeenshire]

WILSON, WILLIAM, master of the Hope of Portsoy, Banffshire, trading between Oporto, Portugal, and Inverness in 1806. [NRS.E504.17.8]

WINCHESTER, JOHN, a shipmaster in Garmouth, Moray, a sasine, 1809. [NRS.RS.Elgin.753]; testament, 1812, Comm. Moray. [NRS]

WISEMAN, JAMES, in Banff, late Lieutenant Colonel of the 91st Regiment of Foot, testament, 1800, Comm. Aberdeen. [NRS]

WISEMAN, JAMES, master of the Brothers Increase of Gardenstown, Banffshire, trading between Easdale and Inverness in 1806. [NRS.E504.17.8]

WISLEY, Reverend GEORGE, in Malta, brother of William Wisley in Nevie, Glen Livet, Banffshire, who died on 16 November 1847. [NRS.S/H.1881]

WOOD, JOHN, son of James Wood and his wife Margaret Barclay, died in Calcutta, India, in 1791. [Cowie gravestone, Kincardineshire]

WOOD, THOMAS, born 2 December 1759, son of James Wood and his wife Margaret Barclay, died in America in 1818. [Fetteresso gravestone, Kincardineshire]

WRIGHT, ALEXANDER MACLEAN, born 7 July 1852 in Elgin, Moray, son of George Wright, was educated at Aberdeen University in 1876, a minister in New Zealand from 1879, died on 16 December 1900. [F.7.605]

WRIGHT, or SIMPSON, BATHIA SOUTAR, daughter of Thomas Wright in Banff, and wife of Alexander Simpson from Macduff in Banffshire, died in Illinois on 20 September 1860. [AJ.24.10.1860]

WRIGHT, JAMES, from Grantown on Spey, Moray, settled in St Thomas parish, South Carolina, probate 12 June 1790, S.C.

WRIGHT, JAMES, born 1818, son of Simon Wright and his wife Margaret Dunnet, died in the West Indies on 22 July 1856. [St Devenick-on-the-hill gravestone]

WYAT, ROBERT, a former minister in Skene, Aberdeenshire, died in Dieppe, France, in 1791. [AJ]

YOUNG, ALEXANDER, son of Charles Young a farmer in Birse, Aberdeenshire, graduated MA from Marischal College in 1851, later a missionary in Kandy, Ceylon. [MCA]

YOUNG, HUGH, second son of James Young the sheriff substitute of Kincardineshire, a merchant who died in New Orleans, Louisiana, on 15 February 1833. [AJ.4449]

YOUNG, JAMES, son of Lieutenant George Young of the Royal Navy in Portsoy, Banffshire, died in St Louis, Missouri, on 9 December 1848. [AJ.5276]

YOUNG, ROBERT, in Elgin, Moray, married Isabella Turburn Johnston, daughter of Hugh Johnston of St John, New Brunswick, in Aberdeenshire on 21 April 1836. [NBRG.22.6.1836]

YOUNGSON, JOHN, from Inverurie, graduated MA from King's College, Aberdeen, I March 1851. [KCA]

YULE, ALEXANDER, in Houseahill, testament, 1790, Comm. Aberdeen. [NRS]

YULE, ALEXANDER, born 1794 in Meikle Rathen, Aberdeenshire, died in Wisconsin on 29 May 1868. [AJ.15.7.1868]

YULE, ALEXANDER, a shipmaster in Fraserburgh, inventory, 1822, Comm. Aberdeen. [NRS]

YULE, Mrs ANN, born 1781, widow of John Yule, from Burnside, Craigievar, Aberdeenshire, died in Virginia Grove, Iowa, on 9 January 1861. [AJ.27.2.1861]

YULE, SAMUEL, from Aberdeenshire, settled in Ashland County, Ohio, in 1836, moved to Red Oak, Indiana, in 1837. [ENES.I.252]

YULL, GEORGE T., from Little Ardo, Aberdeenshire, married Hermin, eldest daughter of George Kosma of Neutra, Hungary, there on 19 January 1862. [AJ.5955]

www.ingramcontent.com/pod-product-compliance
Lightning Source LLC
Chambersburg PA
CBHW050821160426
43192CB00010B/1853